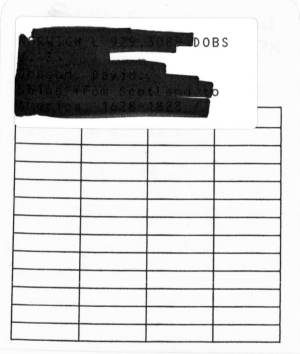

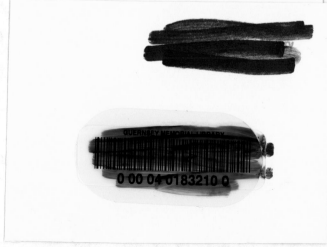

Georgia. Port of *Savannah*

THESE are to certify all whom it may concern, That *William Forrester* ———— Master or Commander of the *Ship Fisher & Friendship* Burthen *100.* Tons or thereabouts, Mounted with *no.* Guns, Navigated with *11.* Men, *Plantation* Built, Registered at *Leith the 26.ᵗʰ January 1771.* Bound for *Leith* ———————— Having on Board

Alexander Thomson Coll.ʳ

Lumber, Enumerated, and Non-enumerated Goods, as ₱. Three Certificates, and a Tobacc Manifest from this.— also a Grou Certificate for Six Hogshead Muscoi Sugar, ₱. brought in said Vep from Grenado's, and not landed her which is now on board. ————

Will.ᵐ Brown comptʳ & Searchʳ

W.ᵐ Haven N. Off.ᵐ

Hath Entered and Cleared at this His Majesty's Custom-House in *Savannah in Georgia* according to Law. ———————— Given under our Hands and Seals of Office, this *Seco* Day of *April* ———— in the *thirteenth* Year of the Reign of our Sovereign Lord GEORGE the Third, King of *Great-Britain, &c.* Annoque Domini, **1773**.

Ships
from SCOTLAND
to AMERICA

1628 – 1828

Volume III

By David Dobson

Copyright © 2004
Genealogical Publishing Co., Inc.
1001 N. Calvert St., Baltimore, Md. 21202
All Rights Reserved.
Library of Congress Catalogue Card Number 2004109124
International Standard Book Number 0-8063-1753-1
Made in the United States of America

INTRODUCTION

One of the more difficult tasks encountered by genealogists in North America is establishing how and when their immigrant ancestor arrived from Scotland. This is particularly true for the seventeenth and eighteenth centuries, periods for which records are far from comprehensive. If the vessel that the immigrant sailed on can be identified, then the ports of arrival and departure may also follow, and in turn this may indicate the locality from which the immigrant originated, thus narrowing the search. Information pertaining to the ship that brought one's immigrant ancestor is an essential feature of a comprehensive family history. What kind of ship was it? What was its tonnage? Where was it registered? Who was the skipper? All these questions are of interest to the family historian and are partially answered in this book.

This book is designed as an aid to the family historian by identifying ships from Scotland to what is now the United States and Canada for the period 1628 to 1828. Evidence of direct shipping between Scotland and the Americas can be established as early as 1600 when the *Grace of God* returned to Dundee from Newfoundland. Links with the West Indies date from 1611 and the voyage of the *Janet of Leith*, and with the Chesapeake with the *Golden Lion of Dundee*, which sailed via London in 1626. All these, however, are believed to have been trading voyages. Emigration to America from Scotland began with the attempt by Sir William Alexander to settle Nova Scotia in the 1620s. It is believed that although there were a number of vessels which could be described as "emigrant ships," the majority of emigrants during our period went on cargo ships. There seems to have been a continuous trickle of emigrants across the Atlantic from the mid-seventeenth century onwards, to staff the tobacco warehouses in Virginia, for example, or as felons banished to the Plantations. Economic forces generally determined emigrant routes from Scotland: ships sailed to Georgia and the Carolinas for cotton and rice, to the Chesapeake for tobacco, to the Canadian Maritimes for timber, and carried with them innumerable emigrants, many as indentured servants. The significant rise in emigration from Great Britain, especially from the Scottish Highlands that occurred in the decade before the American Revolution resulted in the British government maintaining a Register of Emigrants. This, albeit incomplete, covers the period 1773 to 1774 and identifies who emigrated, how they emigrated, why they emigrated, when they emigrated, plus their ports of departure and destination. The only similar large-scale emigration occurred in the years after the end of the Napoleonic Wars when thousands of Scots sailed from the Clyde bound for Canada. Apart from these two periods the picture is far from complete. Passenger arrival records in the United States and Canada are sometimes vague and identify the port of origin as "Scotland" or "North Britain." This is particularly true in the case of emigrant ships that sailed from remote bays or inlets in the Highlands and Islands where the catchment area for the emigrants was highly localized. By the early nineteenth century Greenock had become the major port for emigrants from all over Scotland, but ships did sail from other ports, and their passengers are highly likely to have come from their immediate neighborhoods.

Volume III of *Ships from Scotland to America, 1628–1828* differs from the earlier volumes in that it includes a number of vessels bound from Scotland to the West Indies dating from 1611. Prior to the introduction of the steam ship on the Atlantic from the 1830s, the routes taken by sailing vessels were largely determined by winds and tides. The vast majority of ships leaving the British Isles bound for the Americas headed south to the Azores, Madeira, or the Canary Islands, or even the Cape Verde Islands before turning west towards the Caribbean, and from there north to the mainland colonies. A minority of ships went north via the Orkney Islands and from there to the Canadian Maritimes, Hudson Bay, and sometimes New England. The Scots ships of the period were basically merchant ships, carrying linens, woollens, metal-wares, coal, fish, and provisions to the colonies and returning with raw materials such as sugar, tobacco, cotton, timber, and indigo. Some ships would call at islands such as Barbados, Antigua, Grenada, or Jamaica, to exchange part of their cargoes for sugar and then progress to the American Colonies to obtain other raw materials, at the same time they would disembark passengers at any of these locations. Probably the best account of this traffic occurs in Janet Schaw's *Journal of a Lady of Quality* (1922), which records the voyage of the *Jamaica Packet of Burntisland*, master Thomas Smith, which sailed from Kirkcaldy to Port Brunswick, North Carolina, in June 1775, via the West Indies. Some ships that left Scotland bound for the West Indies returned directly, but others called in at American colonial ports on the return journey. This book also includes a number of early return journeys from America where the record of the outward voyage has not survived.

David Dobson
St. Andrews, Scotland

REFERENCES

ARCHIVES

HBCA = Hudson's Bay Company Archives, Winnipeg
NAS = National Archives of Scotland, Edinburgh
PRO = Public Record Office, London

PUBLICATIONS

AJ = Aberdeen Journal, series
BNL = Boston News Letter, series
CCA = Clyde Commercial Advertiser, series
CM = Caledonian Mercury, series
DPCA = Dundee, Perth, & Cupar Advertiser, series
EdAd = Edinburgh Advertiser, series
EdGaz = Edinburgh Gazette, series
EEC = Edinburgh Evening Courant, series
EWJ = Edinburgh Weekly Journal, series
GaGaz = Georgia Gazette, series
GC = Glasgow Chronicle, series
GCo = Glasgow Courant, series
GMerc = Glasgow Mercury, series
MC = Montrose Chronicle, series
MdGaz = Maryland Gazette, series
PAB = Port Arrivals and Immigrants to Boston, W. H. Whitmore (Baltimore, 1973)
PC = Perth Courier, series
QG = Quebec Gazette, series
QM = Quebec Mercury, series
S = Scotsman, series
SC = Scots Courant, series
SCGaz = South Carolina Gazette, series
VSS = Virginia Slave Trade Statistics, 1698–1775, W. Minchinton (Richmond, 1984)

SHIPS FROM SCOTLAND TO AMERICA, 1628-1828

Volume III

ACADIA, British built, master John Marshall, from
Greenock to Jamaica and Tortula in January 1786.
[NAS.E504.15.42]

ACHILLES, Captain Graham, from Greenock to St Kitts
in December 1758. [AJ#573]

ACHILLES OF BOSTON, a 120 ton snow, master John
Wilson, arrived in Charleston on 25 December
1762 from Glasgow. [PRO.CO5.510]

ACHSAH, arrived in Annapolis, Maryland, in September
1756 from Glasgow. [MdGaz#592]

ACTIVE, master John Scougall, from Leith to Charleston,
South Carolina, in September 1786.
[NAS.E504.22.30]

ADAM AND BETTY OF INVERKEITHING, 160 tons,
master David Inglis, from Leith to Jamaica in
November 1763. [NAS.E504.22.11]

ADDISON, master James Murray, from the Chesapeake
bound for Leith in October 1761. [MdGaz#858]

ADVENTURE OF BOSTON, master John Lowel, arrived
in New Port Glasgow from New England in January

(?) 1720, from there **with passengers** bound for Boston in March 1720. [EEC#186]

ADVENTURE OF AYR, master William Howie, from Greenock to Boston, New England, on 9 March 1728. [EEC#344]

ADVENTURE, Captain Smith, from Glasgow **with passengers** bound for Jamaica in August 1749. [AJ#83]

ADVENTURE, a snow, master James Hamilton, from Leith **with passengers** bound for Kingston, Jamaica, before 1755. [NAS.AC7.47.598]

ADVENTURE OF GREENOCK, 98 tons, master Archibald Yuill, in Charleston, South Carolina, in December 1759. [PRO.CO5.510]

ADVENTURE OF PERTH, master David Robertson, from Dundee to Norfolk, Virginia, 2 October 1771. [NAS.E504.11.7]

ADVENTURE, master Thomas Symmers, from Aberdeen **with passengers** to Barbados, Tobago, and Grenada, on 29 April 1774. [AJ#1360/1373]

ADVENTURE OF GREENOCK, Plantation Built, master Moses Crawford, from Greenock to Grenada in April 1776; master Andrew McNeill, from Greenock to Barbados in November 1784; from Greenock to Barbados in June 1785; from Greenock to Barbados in October 1785. [NAS.E504.15.26/40/41/42]

ADVENTURE, a 250 ton brig, master D. Wallace, from Greenock **with passengers**, bound for Kingston, Jamaica, in October 1821. [EEC#17209]

ADVENTURE, a brig, master Thomas Adamson, from Dundee **with passengers** to New York on 15 September 1827. [DPCA#1307]

ADVICE, Captain Webster, from Dundee to Miramachi in August 1808. [DPCA#316]

AEOLUS, master John Rankin, from Port Glasgow to Barbados in March 1774; master Walter Wright, from Port Glasgow to Jamaica in December 1783. [NAS.E504.28.23/36]

AGNES OF GLASGOW, master Robert Arthur, from Greenock to Boston, New England, on 13 March 1728; arrived in Greenock on 14 December from Virginia. [EEC#448/579]

AID, 450 tons, master George Crockett, from Leith **with passengers** bound for Quebec on 25 May 1828. [S.XII.864]

AJAX OF GREENOCK, master John Dean, from Greenock to Grenada in June 1776. [NAS.E504.15.26]

AKERS, master James Poe, from Greenock to St Kitts in March 1781. [NAS.E504.15.33]

ALBANY OF GLASGOW, master Andrew Giles, arrived in Greenock from Virginia on 9 September 1728; from Greenock via Rotterdam to Virginia 20 November 1728. [EEC#543/565]

ALBANY, master David Johnston, from Port Glasgow to Virginia in January 1784, also in August 1785. [NAS.E504.28.37/39][MdGaz#1075]

ALBION OF GLASGOW, master John Campbell, from Greenock to St Kitts in January 1775 and in January 1776; master John McGregor, from Greenock to St Kitts in January 1777; from Greenock to St Kitts in March 1778; master John Robertson, from Greenock to Barbados in May 1779; from Greenock to St Lucia in August 1781; from Greenock to St Lucia in March 1782; master Walter Buchanan, from Greenock to Barbados in November 1783; master John McMillan, from

Greenock to Jamaica in November 1784; from Greenock to Grenada in October 1785. [NAS.E504.15.25/26/27/29/31/34/35/38/40/41]

ALBION OF DUNDEE, Captain Kidd, from Dundee to Quebec, *with 65 passengers from Perthshire* in 1809. [DPL]

ALDIE, master Peter Brown, from Leith *with passengers* bound for Grenada on 7 December 1777. [AJ#1558]

ALERT OF ABERDEEN, master Andrew Johnston, from Aberdeen *with 2 passengers* bound for Quebec, arrived there in May 1812. [QM.30.5.1812]

ALEXANDER OF GLASGOW, a 40 ton brigantine, master William Gammell, from Irvine via Barbados to South Carolina, arrived in Charleston on 22 February 1730. [PRO.CO5/509]

ALEXANDER OF BOSTON, master Alexander Ross, from Kirkwall to Falmouth, New England, 19 September 1753. [NAS.E504.26.2]

ALEXANDER, master James Hamilton, from Leith to Annapolis, Maryland, in October 1756. [NAS.E504.22.7]

ALEXANDER, master Robert Peacock, from Oxford, Maryland, to Glasgow on November 1765; arrived in Baltimore, Maryland, in December 1766 from Glasgow. [MdGaz#Suppl.441; #1109]

ALEXANDER OF GREENOCK, master Neil Campbell, from Greenock to Jamaica in January 1776; master John Baine, from Greenock to Jamaica in January 1778; from Greenock to Jamaica in February 1779; master John Baine, from Greenock to Jamaica in November 1779; from Greenock to Jamaica in January 1781; from Greenock to Jamaica in January 1782; from Greenock to Jamaica in January 1783; master Robert Raeside, from

Greenock to Jamaica in February 1784; from
Greenock to Jamaica in March 1785; from
Greenock to Jamaica in March 1786.
[NAS.E504.15.26/29/30/32 /33/35/37/38/40/42];
master Robert Raeside, from Greenock to Martha
Brae, Jamaica, in January 1787, *"a house
carpenter (for) Jamaica, may apply"*.
[GMerc:12.1786]

ALEXANDER, master John Baine, from Greenock to
Jamaica in February 1777. [NAS.E504.15.27]

ALEXANDER AND JAMES, master Stephen Rowan,
from Greenock to Barbados in October 1755; from
Greenock to St Kitts on 23 October 1756; from
Greenock to St Kitts in February 1758.
[NAS.E504.15.7][AJ#460/529]

ALFRED, Captain Crawford, from Greenock to Jamaica
on 30 January 1819; Captain Spencer, from
Greenock to St Kitts on 17 May 1819.
[EEC#16797/16842]]

ALLAN, galley, master James Craigie, from Leith *with
passengers* bound for South Carolina in July 1728.
[EEC#506]

AMELIA OF NEW YORK, master Robert Pickeman, from
Kirkwall to New York 24 June 1754.
[NAS.E504.26.2]

AMELIA, master Robert Lindsay, from Greenock to St
Kitts in October 1781. [NAS.E504.15.35]

AMERICA OF GLASGOW, master James Scott, from
Greenock *with passengers* bound for Virginia in
November 1736. [EEC#1980]

AMERICA, master James Gammell, from Greenock to
Guadaloupe in November 1759. [NAS.E504.15.9]

AMETHYST OF ABERDEEN, master Alexander Gray,
from Aberdeen *with 29 passengers* bound for

Halifax, Nova Scotia, in March 1815.
[NAS.E504.1.25]

AMITY OF WHITEHAVEN, master John Sharp. arrived in
Greenock on 9 October 1728 from Virginia.
[EEC#554]

AMITY OF GLASGOW, 56 tons, master George Blair,
arrived in the Lower James River, Virginia, on 16
February 1734 via Jamaica, [PRO.CO5.1443];
master James Weir, from Greenock to Jamaica on
25 April 1741, [CM#3290]; from Port Glasgow to
Philadelphia in January 1744; Captain Weir, from
Glasgow via Cork to Jamaica, captured and taken
to Havanna in 1745, [SM.VII.594]; from Port
Glasgow **with passengers** bound for Jamaica on 1
November 1748, [AJ#40]; Captain Aitken, from
Greenock to Jamaica in December 1749, [AJ#104];
master Robert How, from Port Glasgow to Boston
in March 1751 [NAS.E504.29/1, 5]

AMITY OF GLASGOW, a 100 ton snow, master Peter
Cochrane, arrived in Charleston, South Carolina,
on 10 January 1767 from Glasgow. [PRO.CO5.511]

AMITY, Captain Aitken, from Greenock to Jamaica in
November 1748 and in December 1749.
[AJ#48/104]

ANDERSON, master William Hamilton, from the
Chesapeake bound for Glasgow in October 1761.
[MdGaz#858]

ANDERSON, master Allan Hervey, from Greenock to St
Kitts in November 1781. [NAS.E504.15.35]

ANN GALLEY OF INVERNESS, master James Dawling,
from Scotland to Barbados in 1715 and 1717.
[NAS.E508.9.6/10.6]

ANNE OF EDINBURGH, master James Blair, from Leith
bound for New England in October 1736.
[EEC#1976]

ANN OF GLASGOW, master John Smith, from Greenock to Jamaica in June 1745. [NAS.E504.15.2]; 200 tons, from Port Glasgow via Cork *with persons willing to indent for 4 years in Jamaica* to Jamaica in September 1746. [CM#4027]

ANN, master John Wilson, from Irvine bound for Virginia in January 1762. [NAS.E504.18.5]

ANN, master Joshia Aitken, from Leith to Boston in May 1764. [NAS.E504.22.11]

ANN, master William Mackie, from Greenock to Barbados and Antigua in May 1783. [NAS.E504.15.38]

ANN, master Alexander Huie, from Port Glasgow to Virginia in February 1784; from Port Glasgow to Virginia in March 1785; from Port Glasgow to Virginia in February 1786. [NAS.E504.28.36/38/40]

ANN, a brig, Captain Barry, from Greenock *with passengers* to New York on November 1824. [DPCA#1158]

ANNA OF GLASGOW, a galley, master James Barclay, from Glasgow to Barbados and return by 1715. [NAS.AC8.196]

ANNA OF ABERDEEN, master James Ferguson, from Montrose via Aberdeen to Virginia in April 1758. [AJ#17]

ANNABELLA, a brig, from Campbeltown, Argyll, *with 70 passengers* bound for the Island of St John's in the Bay of St Lawrence, 1770. [NAS.RH1.2.933/ii]

ANN ELIZABETH, a 140 ton brig, Captain Morgan, from Dundee *with passengers* to New York in March 1817. [DPCA#761]

ANN AND ELIZABETH OF GLASGOW, master Alexander Muir, from Greenock to Virginia on 5 April 1721. [EEC#365]

ANN AND MARGARET OF LEVEN, master James Black, from Scotland to Virginia in 1722. [NAS.E508.16.6]

ANNA OF GLASGOW, master James Barclay, from Barbados to Glasgow by 1715. [NAS.AC8.196]

ANNA MARIA OF MONTROSE, 180 tons, master John Scott, arrived in Charleston in 1736 via London. [PRO.CO5.510]

ANNE OF INVERNESS, from Inverness via Cork to Barbados and Virginia in 1716. [NAS.AC9.702]

ANNE, a snow, master Neil Jamieson, arrived in Charleston, South Carolina, in April 1756 from Glasgow. [SCGaz#1140]

ANSLIE OF LEITH, 80 tons, master John Hay, arrived in Charleston on 27 November 1735. [PRO.CO5.509]

ANTELOPE OF ABERDEEN, from Aberdeen to Virginia in 1711. [Scots Courant, 26.5.1711]

ANTELOPE, a snow, master Robert Hastie, arrived in Annapolis, Maryland, in July 1761 from Glasgow. [MdGaz.845]

ANTELOPE, master James Gordon, from Port Glasgow to St Kitts in March 1784. [NAS.E504.28.37]

ANTIGUA PACKET OF ABERDEEN, master Lewis Gellie, from Aberdeen *with passengers* bound for Antigua in September 1751; from Aberdeen to Antigua in February 1753. [AJ#192/260]

ANTIGUA PACKET, master John Carson, from Port Glasgow to Antigua in May 1785. [NAS.E504.22.39]

ARCHIBALD OF GREENOCK, master Robert Watson, from Greenock via Madeira to Barbados on 31 December 1748. [AJ#50][NAS.E504.15.4]

ARDENT, Captain Paterson, from Greenock to Grenada on 9 March 1819. [EEC#16814]

ARGYLE, master William Watson, from Greenock *with passengers* to Jamaica on 15 October 1734, *'any tradesmen, such as house or mill wrights, coopers, masons, bricklayers, tailors or blacksmiths, who will indent for 5 years...'*. [CM#2264]

ARGYLE, Captain Montgomerie, from Greenock to Antigua on 2 May 1747. [CM#4146]; from Greenock via Cork to the West Indies in January 1749, [AJ#57]; from Greenock via Cork to Antigua on 29 September 1750, [AJ#145]

ARGYLE OF GREENOCK, master Charles Cunningham, arrived in Savanna, Georgia, on 25 January 1766 via Jamaica. [PRO.CO5.710][GaGaz]

ARGYLL, Captain Montgomerie, from Greenock via Cork to Antigua in November 1748; from Greenock to St Kitts in February 1752; from Greenock to St Kitts in February 1754; master Charles Cunningham, from Greenock to Jamaica in January 1765. [AJ#48/214/319] [NAS.E504.15.12]

ARGYLL OF CAMPBELTOWN, a snow, master Robert Fairy, to Philadelphia in July 1754. [NAS.AC20.2.14/4]

ARIEL, a 234 ton brig, master A. Mackinley, from Greenock *with passengers* to St Thomas and Savannah in 1823; master Allan Mackinlay, from Glasgow *with passengers* bound for Charleston and Savannah in November 1824. [DPCA#1109/1160]

ASTREA, Captain Barclay, from Dundee via Newcastle bound for Baltimore and Richmond in March 1824. [DPCA#1130]

ATALANTA, master Robert Kerr, from Greenock to St Kitts in March 1782. [NAS.E504.15.35]

ATLANTIC, Captain Balfour, from Dundee to St Andrews, New Brunswick, on 25 July 1825. [DPCA#1200]

AUGUSTUS CAESAR, master John Coutts, from Aberdeen *with passengers* via London to Jamaica in July 1753; from Aberdeen *with* passengers to Kingston, Jamaica, in August 1754; from Aberdeen *with passengers* to Kingston, Jamaica, in August 1755. [AJ#284/337/382/397]

AURORA OF GREENOCK, 90 tons, master Archibald Fisher, arrived in Charleston on 6 December 1766 from Glasgow; master Gregor McGregor, from Greenock to Grenada in January 1776; master Neil Campbell, from Greenock to Jamaica in December 1783; master Archibald Campbell, from Greenock to Jamaica in November 1784; from Greenock to Jamaica in November 1785. [PRO.CO5.511] [E504.15.26/38/40/42]; master Archibald Campbell, from Greenock bound for Martha Brae, Jamaica, in December 1786, *"a house carpenter, young and well recommended, that will bind himself for four or five years to a gentleman's employ in Jamaica, may apply"*. [GMerc:12.1786]

AURORA, master John Montgomerie, from Port Glasgow to Tortula in November 1783. [NAS.E504.28.36]

AURORA, 229 tons, master Thomas Boyd, from Glasgow *with passengers* to New York in October 1808. [DPCA#321]

AURORA, a 196 ton brig, Captain Lawson, from Dundee *with passengers* to Richmond, Norfolk, and Philadelphia in 1823. [DPCA#1077]

BACHELORS OF LONDON, 160 tons, master Alexander Urquhart, arrived in Charleston on 10 March 1765 from Leith. [PRO.CO5.511]

BACHELOR OF LEITH, 160 ton, Plantation built, master Alexander Urquhart, from Leith to Charleston, South Carolina, on 20 December 1765; Alexander Ramage, from Leith to Cape Fear in August 1773. [NAS.E504.22.12/18]

BACHELOR OF DYSART, Plantation built, 160 tons, George Barclay, from Leith to Edenton, North Carolina, in January 1775; from Leith to Grenada in March 1776. [NAS.E504.22.18/20]

BALTIC, a 170 ton brig, master Alexander Caird, from Dundee *with passengers* bound for New York in January 1808; master James Morrison, from Dundee *with passengers* to New York on 15 September 1827. [DPCA#284/1307]

BARBADOS, British built, master Andrew McNeil, from Greenock to Barbados in May 1786. [NAS.E504.15.42]

BARBARA OF LONDON, master William Epsom, from Aberdeen *with 4 passengers* to Quebec in March 1812. [NAS.E504.1.24]

BARBARY OF LEITH, a 60 ton pink, master Samuel Scollay, in Charleston, South Carolina, in April 1731. [PRO.CO5.509]

BARRINGTON, master James Boutcher, from Greenock to Antigua and St Kitts in July 1779. [NAS.E504.15.31]; master Hector Stevenson, from Leith *with passengers* to New York in November 1795. [AJ#2491]

BASSETERRE, Captain MacMorland, from Greenock to Savannah, Georgia, on 14 February 1819. [EEC#16803]

BEATTIE OF BO'NESS, master John Finlayson, from Greenock to Antigua by 1712. [NAS.AC8/139]

BEAUFORT, Captain Kelburn, from Greenock to St Kitts on 16 June 1755; from Glasgow to St Kitts in March 1756; Captain Golkison, from Greenock to St Kitts in December 1758. [AJ#389/425/571]

BEAVER, master J. Richards, from Gravesend via Orkney to Eastmain, Moose, and Albany, Hudson's Bay, in 1788, 1791, and 1792. [HBCA#2M1]

BEGGARS BENNISON, master George Affleck, arrived in Savannah, Georgia, on 1 January 1768 from Dunbar, East Lothian, [GaGaz:6.1.1768]; master James Gardner, from Irvine, Ayrshire, to Georgia in September 1771; master Patrick Muir, from Irvine bound for Georgia in November 1772. [NAS.E504.18.7/8]

BELFAST, Captain Gibbons, from the Clyde to New York, lost at sea 200 miles off New York in December 1827. [DPCA#1332]

BELINA, a 155 ton brigantine, master D. Mitchell, from Dundee to New York in December 1827. [DPCA#1322]

BELL OF GLASGOW, 90 tons, master David Peter, in Charleston, South Carolina, in May 1762; master Richard Hunter, arrived in Charleston on 15 December 1762 from Glasgow. [PRO.CO5.510]

BELL, master Robert Adams, from Greenock to St Kitts in January 1765. [NAS.E504.12]

BELL OF GREENOCK, master Allan Speir, from Greenock to Barbados in February 1776. [NAS.E504.15.26]

BELL, master Thomas Duncan, from Port Glasgow to Barbados in March 1784. [NAS.E504.28.37]

BELL OF GREENOCK, 173 tons, British built, master John Cathcart, from Greenock to St Kitts and Jamaica in September 1785; from Greenock to Tortula in September 1786; from Greenock *with 15 passengers* to Jamaica on 21 August 1787. [NAS.E504.15.41/43/45]

BELL, from Greenock *with passengers* bound for the West Indies 10 January 1795. [EEC:25.12.1794]

BELLONA, master Arthur Ryburn, from Greenock to Tortula in October 1782. [NAS.E504.15.37]

BELLONA, Captain Taylor, from Dundee via St Andrews, New Brunswick, to New York in September 1808. [DPCA#315]

BELMONT, master James Yuil, from Greenock to Grenada in November 1784. [NAS.E504.15.40]

BENJAMIN OF GLASGOW, from Port Glasgow to the West Indies on 7 August 1681. [NAS.E72,19.4]

BETSY OF LEITH, 130 tons, master Charles Cunningham, from Leith to Guadaloupe in October 1759; from Leith to Antigua in October 1760; master Henry Steel, from Leith to Grenada in February 1775. [NAS.E504.22.9/10/19]

BETSEY, master John Barber, from Greenock to Grenada in April 1776; from Greenock to Grenada in October 1776; from Greenock to Grenada in December 1777; from Greenock to Grenada in October 1778; master Robert Douglas, from Port Glasgow to Maryland in October 1783; master Robert McLeish, from Greenock to Grenada in April 1784; from Greenock to Grenada in February 1785. [NAS.E504.15.26/28/30/38/40] [NAS,E504.22.36]

BETSY, master Andrew Anderson, from the Chesapeake bound for Glasgow in October 1761. [MdGaz#858]

BETSY OF GREENOCK, a 75 ton brigantine, master Duncan Campbell, arrived in Charleston, South Carolina, on 24 November 1763 from Glasgow. [PRO.CO5.511]

BETSY, master Peter Brown, from Port Glasgow to Virginia in July 1785. [NAS.E504.22.39]

BETSEY, a brig, master Peter Nucator, from Dundee to St Andrews, New Brunswick, in July 1808. [DPCA#309]

BETSY AND SALLY, Captain Maxwell, from Greenock to Antigua in August 1752. [AJ#241]

BETSY CAMPBELL, master John Baine, from Port Glasgow to St Vincent in October 1773, [NAS.E504.28.22]

BETTY OF GLASGOW, master James Crawford, from Greenock to Virginia on 17 February 1741. [CM#3262]

BETTY OF METHIL, 80 tons, Plantation built, master Robert Salmon, from Kirkcaldy, Fife, to Boston, New England, 10 July 1753. [NAS.E504.20.3]

BETTY, master Robert Watson, from Greenock to Jamaica in April 1755; Captain Watson, from Greenock to Antigua on 8 May 1756. [NAS.E504.15.7][AJ#437]

BETTY, master William Gray, from Greenock to St Kitts in April 1755. [NAS.E504.15.7]

BETTY, master Colin Douglas, from the Clyde to Jamaica, arrived in St Kitts by 10 April 1759. [AJ#593]

BETTY OF GREENOCK, a 75 ton brigantine, master Duncan Campbell, arrived in Charleston, South Carolina, on 29 August 1764 via St Kitts. [PRO.CO5.510]

BETTY OF LEITH, a 80 ton snow, master Angus McLarty, from Leith in March 1766 bound for Charleston, South Carolina, arrived there on 5 November 1766 from Glasgow; from Leith *with 120 passengers* bound for Cape Fear, North Carolina, arrived in Charleston, in September 1769. [PRO.CO5.511][SCGaz.14.9.1769][NAS.E504.22.12]

BETTY OF PORT GLASGOW, master John Fullarton, from Port Glasgow via Waterford to St Lucia and St Thomas in 1782. [NAS.AC7.64]

BETTY AND JANE, Captain Glen, from Greenock to Barbados on 12 April 1746. [CM#3982]

BETTY AND JENNY, Captain MacClow, from Irvine bound for Barbados in 1746, captured by the French and taken to Martinique. [SM.IX.97]

BETTY AND MARY OF ABERDEEN, Captain Gelly, from Aberdeen to Antigua in February 1750. [AJ#113]

BETTY CATHCART OF GREENOCK, 270 tons, master John Cathcart, from Greenock *with 30 passengers* to Jamaica on 28 August 1788. [NAS.E504.15.49]

BINNING, master Robert Steel, from Port Glasgow to Virginia in July 1752. [NAS.E504.28/5]

BIRD, master John McDonald, from Greenock to Jamaica in October 1779; from Greenock to Jamaica in January 1782; master John Galt, from Greenock to Jamaica in January 1783; from Greenock to Jamaica in October 1783; from Port Glasgow to Newfoundland in July 1785. [NAS.E504.15.32/35/37/38][NAS.E504.22.39]

BLACKBURN, a schooner, master Edward Morrison, arrived in Boston, New England, on 19 September 1766 *with passengers* from Glasgow. [PAB]

BLACK PRINCE OF PORTSMOUTH, an 86 ton brigantine, master Henry Freer, arrived in Charleston, South Carolina, on 21 November 1763 from Dunbar. [PRO.CO5.511]

BLAGROVE OF GREENOCK, master James Noble, from Greenock to Jamaica in January 1776; from Greenock to Jamaica in October 1776; from Greenock to Jamaica in October 1777; from Greenock to Jamaica in October 1778; master Archibald Thomson, from Greenock to Jamaica in November 1779. [NAS.E504.15.26/27/28/30/32]

BLAKELY, Captain Burril, from Dundee to Charleston, South Carolina, on 28 October 1823. [DPCA#1109]

BLANDFORD, master Peter Bryson, from Greenock to Grenada in December 1764; master Andrew Troop, from Port Glasgow to Virginia in July 1784 and in June 1785. [NAS.E504.15.12/22.39]

BOGLE OF GLASGOW, master James Fleming, from Port Glasgow to Virginia in February 1751. [NAS.E504.28/5]; master James Montgomery, arrived in Annapolis, Maryland, in July 1755 from Glasgow, from Annapolis bound for Glasgow in November 1755. [MdGaz#534/551]

BOLIVAR, a 236 ton brig, master James MacDonald, from Dundee *with passengers* to New York in February 1826. [DPCA#1230]

BOLLING, Captain James Porteous, arrived in Annapolis, Maryland, in July 1761 from Glasgow. [MdGaz.846]

BON ACCORD OF ABERDEEN, BB, 50 tons, master William Ross, arrived in Aberdeen on 13 August 1743 from Port Oxford, Maryland; from Aberdeen to Virginia in March 1744. [NAS.E504.1.1]

BONADVENTURE OF GREENOCK, master James Shaw, from Greenock to Jamaica in March 1747. [NAS.E504.15.3][CM#4143]

BONNY LASS OF LIVINGSTOUN, master Hugh Wilson, from Irvine, Ayrshire, bound for Quebec in February 1765. [NAS.E504.18.5]

BOWLING OF GLASGOW, 140 tons, Robert Douglas, from Leith to Virginia June 1757. [NAS.E504.22.7]

BOWMAN, master Humphrey Taylor, from Port Glasgow to Barbados in March 1775. [NAS.E504.28.24]

BOYD GALLEY, master James Main, from Port Glasgow to Virginia in February 1745; master John Douglas, from Port Glasgow to Virginia in February 1752 [NAS.E504.28/1, 4, 5]

BOYD, master James Boyd, from Port Glasgow to Virginia in July 1784, in March 1785, in August 1785, and March 1786. [NAS.E504.22.37/38/39/40]

BRAYTON, master John Harrison, from Greenock to St Vincent in March 1785. [NAS.E504.15.40]

BRILLIANT, master Robert Bennet, from Port Glasgow to Barbados in October 1774. [NAS.E504.28.23]

BROTHERS OF GOUROCK, a 50 ton brigantine, master Robert Arthur, arrived in Charleston, South Carolina, on 24 March 1727 from Greenock. [PRO.CO5/509]

BRISCOE, Captain McKirdy, arrived in Maryland in 1770 from Glasgow. [MdGaz#1289]

BRITANNIA, master Archibald Orr, from Annapolis, Maryland, to Glasgow in September 1753. [MdGaz#435]

BRITANNIA OF GLASGOW, master Archibald McLarty, from Greenock to Jamaica in February 1767; from

Greenock *with passengers* bound for Kingston, Jamaica, in February 1767; master William Scott, arrived in Maryland *with 100 passengers, tradesmen, farmers, etc* in October 1772 from Port Glasgow; master John Watson, arrived in Annapolis, Maryland in February 1775 from Greenock; master David Scott, from Greenock to Jamaica in January 1777; from Greenock to Jamaica in January 1778; master Walter Buchanan, from Greenock to St Vincent in February 1779; from Greenock to Tobago in January 1781; from Greenock to Jamaica in January 1782. [AJ#991] [NAS.E504.15.13/27/28/30/33/35] [MdGaz#1415/1533]

BRITISH KING, a 283 ton snow, master James Moncrieff, from Dundee *with passengers* to New York in August 1825; master John Young, from Dundee *with passengers* to Quebec and Montreal in March 1826; master John Gellatly, from Dundee to Quebec and Montreal on 28 March 1828. [DPCA#1201/1230/1335]

BROTHERS OF GLASGOW, master Robert Rae, arrived in Greenock on 9 September 1728 from Virginia. [EEC#543]

BROTHERS OF GOUROCK, a 50 ton brigantine, master Robert Arthur, arrived in Charleston, South Carolina, on 24 March 1727 from Greenock. [PRO.CO5.509]

BROTHERS OF GREENOCK, Captain Alexander, from Greenock to Barbados on 20 April 1752; master Moses Cunningham from Greenock to Tobago and Pensacola in June 1777. [AJ#226][NAS.E504.15.27]

BROTHERS OF SWANSEY, 120 tons, master Patrick Bogle, arrived in Charleston, South Carolina, on 31 January 1763 from Glasgow, also on 10 January 1766 from Glasgow. [PRO.CO5.510/511]

BROTHERS' BROTHER OF ROTTERDAM, Captain Arnot, at Leith in July 1747 *with 230 Palatines* bound for Philadelphia. [CM#4180]

BROUGHTY CASTLE, an 80 ton brig, master Andrew Law, from Dundee *with passengers* to New York in August 1827. [DPCA#1307]

BRUTUS, a 256 ton brig, master John Keillor, from Dundee to Charleston and Savannah in July 1827. [DPCA#1298]

BUCKSKIN, master Henry Kinnamond, from Port Glasgow to North Carolina in September 1784. [NAS.E504.28.37]

BUTTERFLY OF GLASGOW, master Robert Lyon, from Greenock to Jamaica in August 1743. [NAS.E504.15.1]

BYRD, master Archibald Bog, from Greenock to Nevis and St Kitts in January 1767. [NAS.E504.15.13]

CAESAR OF GLASGOW, 99 tons, master Richard Hunter, in Charleston, South Carolina, during January 1762. [PRO.CO5.510]

CAESAR, master Duncan McLean, from Port Glasgow to Jamaica in October 1772, from Port Glasgow to Jamaica, Tobago and Grenada in May 1773, [NAS.E504.28.21/22]

CAESAR OF GREENOCK, master John Forrest, from Greenock to Barbados in May 1779. [NAS.E504.15.31]

CALEDONIA OF GLASGOW, master Alexander McKinlay, from Greenock to Jamaica in February 1776; master George Orr, from Greenock to Antigua in January 1781; master Lewis Colquhoun, from Greenock via Madeira to Jamaica in December 1783. [NAS.E504.15.26/33/38]

CAMBRIA OF ABERDEEN, master James Pirie, from Aberdeen *with 33 passengers* bound for Halifax, Nova Scotia, and Quebec in May 1812. [AJ: 29.1.1812; NAS.E504.1.24]

CAMDEN, master Benjamin Bell, from Gravesend via Orkney to Moose, Hudson's Bay, in 1824, 1825, and 1826. [HBCA#2M3/4]

CAMILLUS, master Norman Peck, from Greenock *with passengers* to New York on 10 October 1825. [DPCA#1200]

CAROLINA, master John Kennedy, to Guinea and Maryland before 1770. [NAS.AC7.53]

CAROLINA, master John Gardner, from Port Glasgow to Charleston, South Carolina, in September 1784. [NAS.E504.28.37]

CAROLINA OF ABERDEEN, master Alexander Duncan, from Aberdeen *with 24 passengers* bound for Quebec in April 1815. [NAS.E504,1.25]

CARRIERE OF GLASGOW, master James McLeish, from Greenock to Barbados in April 1783; from Greenock to Barbados in October 1783; master Richard Brown, from Greenock to Grenada in September 1784; master James McLeish from Greenock *with passengers* to Grenada in August 1786. [NAS.E504.15.37/38/42][GMerc]

CARY, Captain Tucker, from Glasgow bound for Virginia, captured by the French but ransomed for £2500, in 1758. [SM.20.275]; master John Geills, from the Chesapeake to Glasgow in October 1761. [MdGaz#858]

CASSANDRA, Captain McMillan, from Greenock to Jamaica in March 1748, [CM#4277]; from Greenock to Jamaica in December 1749, [AJ#104]; Captain Hutchison, from Greenock via Cork bound for Jamaica on 29 September 1750, [AJ#145]; master Alexander Hutchison, from Port Glasgow to Philadelphia and Jamaica in August 1751; from Greenock to Philadelphia and Jamaica in September 1754. [NAS.E504.28/5][AJ#192/350]

CASSANDRA, master John Cunningham, from Port Glasgow via Cork to St Kitts in September 1772; from Port Glasgow to St Kitts in October 1773; from Port Glasgow to St Kitts in October 1774; from Port Glasgow to St Kitts in October 1775. [NAS.E504.28.21/22/23/24]; master William Dunlop, from Greenock to Antigua in November 1782. [NAS.E504.15.37]

CASTLE SEMPLE, master Alexander McKinlay, from Greenock to Grenada in March 1778; from Greenock to Grenada in February 1779; from Greenock to Jamaica. and St Kitts in January 1782; from Greenock to Jamaica in September 1782; from Greenock to Jamaica in October 1783; from Greenock to Jamaica in October 1784; master Walter Buchanan, from Greenock to Jamaica in November 1785. [NAS.E504.15.29/30/35/36/38/42]

CATHCART OF GLASGOW, master Robert Patterson, arrived in Greenock on 14 October 1728 from Virginia. [EEC#556]

CATHCART, a snow, master John Smith, from Greenock to Jamaica in December 1758; from Greenock to Jamaica in January 1760, [NAS.E504.15.9]; master William Gilkison, from Glasgow, arrived at Nanjemoy, Maryland, in May 1765. [MdGaz#1045]

CATHERINE OF LONDONDERRY, arrived in Somerset County, Maryland, in 1692 from Scotland. [SPAWI.1692.2295]

CATHERINE OF WHITEHAVEN, from Greenock to Virginia on 25 November 1715. [GCo#2]

CATHERINE OF GLASGOW, a 100 ton snow, master Archibald McMillan, arrived in Nottingham on the Patuxent River, Maryland, from Glasgow in May 1761, from Nottingham to Glasgow in 1761; master John Love, arrived in Charleston, South Carolina, on 8 April 1763 from Glasgow; arrived in Charleston on 22 December 1763 from Greenock; master Hugh Morris, arrived in Boston on 29 August 1768 *with passengers* from Glasgow. [MdGaz.#835/836][PRO.CO5.510][PAB]

CATHERINE, master Robert Speir, from Greenock to Jamaica and Grenada in January 1778. [NAS.E504.15.29]

CATHERINE OF GREENOCK, master Alexander Murdoch, from Greenock to Nevis in March 1779. [NAS.E504.15.30]

CATHERINE OF LEITH, British built,150 tons, master Andrew Mason, from Leith to Grenada and Tobago in April 1783; from Leith to Grenada in January 1785. [NAS.E504.22.27/29]

CATO, master Andrew Lee, from Greenock to Barbados in October 1778. [NAS,E504.15.30]

CATO, a 197 ton brigantine, master David Ritchie, from Dundee to New York on 28 March 1828. [DPCA#1334/1341]

CECILIA, master William Watson, from Greenock to Grenada in March 1778. [NAS.E504.15.29]

CENTURION OF ABERDEEN, master James Morrison, from Aberdeen *with 18 passengers* bound for Halifax, Nova Scotia, in April 1811. [NAS.E504.1.24]

CERES, master George Jamieson, from Port Glasgow to Newfoundland in March 1784. [NAS.E504.28.37]

CERES, a brig, master Thomas Ramsay, from Gravesend via Orkney to Churchill, York Factory, Hudson's Bay, and return in 1802, 1803, and 1804. [HBCA#2M5/6]

CERVANTES, Captain Wright, from Greenock to Kingston, Jamaica, on 2 February 1819. [EEC#16797]

CHAMPION OF LEITH, 130 tons, master Robert Spears, from Leith to Jamaica in October 1774; from Leith to Jamaica in November 1775. [NAS.E504.22.19/20]

CHANCE OF KIRKWALL, 160 tons, master George Smith, arrived in Charleston on 19 January 1758 from Orkney; in Charleston, South Carolina, during February 1760; in Charleston February 1762; arrived in Charleston on 18 November 1762 from Orkney; arrived in Charleston on 29 November 1763 via London and Philadelphia; arrived in Charleston on 5 March 1766 via Cadiz. [PRO.CO5.510/511]

CHANCE, master John McWhae, from Greenock *with 13 passengers* bound for Antigua in August 1775. [PRO.T47/12]; master William McLennan, from Greenock to Jamaica in December 1776; master Thomas Boyd, from Greenock to Barbados in October 1784. [NAS.E504.15.27/40]

CHARLES OF CHARLESTON, master James Reid, in Leith during May 1737. [Edinburgh Burgess Register]

CHARLES OF LEITH, 50 tons, master David Ogilvy, from Leith to Quebec in January 1764. [NAS.E504.22.11]

CHARLOTTE, master Joshua Turstall, from Gravesend via Orkney to Churchill and Moose, Hudson's Bay, and return in 1775 and 1778. [HBCA#2M6]

CHARMING JEANNIE, master John Bannatyne, from Greenock to Jamaica in February 1767. [NAS.E504.15.13]

CHARMING LILLIE OF GLASGOW, master David Cunningham, from Port Glasgow to Virginia in December 1748 and in February 1751. [NAS.E504.28/4, 5]

CHARMING SALLY OF NEW YORK, master William Heysham, from Kirkwall, Orkney, to New York 13 May 1754. [E504.26.2]

CHARMING SALLY, a snow, arrived in Annapolis, Maryland, in December 1758 from Glasgow. [MdGaz#718]

CHARMING SALLY, Captain Taylor, from Stromness, Orkney, to New York on 14 July 1763. [AJ#812]

CHRISTIAN OF LEITH, master Alexander Hutton, from Leith to Barbados by 1720. [NAS.AC9.713]

CHRISTIAN OF FORT WILLIAM, master Hugh Hill, from Greenock to Virginia on 5 April 1721. [EEC#365]

CHRISTIAN OF LEITH, a 95 ton snow, master James Hamilton, arrived in Annapolis, Maryland, in February 1757 from Leith; master Henry Shiell, arrived in Charleston, South Carolina, on 19 March 1759 from Dublin; master Henry Steel, in Charleston in April 1760; from Leith to Grenada in March 1764.
[MdGaz#615][PRO.CO5.510][NAS.E504.22.11]

CHRISTIAN, master John Mackie, from Greenock to Antigua and Tortula in December 1781. [NAS.E504.15.35]

CHRISTIAN AND KAREN OF TRONTHEIM, master Andreas Anderson, from Greenock to St Thomas, Danish West Indies, in September 1782. [NAS.E504.15.36]

CHRISTIE OF ABERDEEN, a 100 ton brigantine, master Robert Gill, from Aberdeen *with passengers* to Jamaica and the Grenades on 30 January 1767; from Aberdeen to Jamaica in October 1767; master George Craik, from Aberdeen *with passengers* to Tobago, Grenada and Kingston, Jamaica, in September 1772; from Aberdeen on 28 December 1773, arrived in Antigua on 24 February 1774 *with passengers* from Aberdeen.
[AJ#990/1035/1287/1356/1374]

CHRISTIE, master Duncan Weir, from Greenock to Dominica in May 1777. [NAS.E504.15.27]

CHRISTINA OF GLASGOW, master David McKay, from Greenock to Jamaica in March 1777; master Robert Bain, from Greenock to Jamaica in February 1778; from Greenock to Jamaica in February 1779; from Greenock to Jamaica in January 1781; master Thomas Hastie, from Greenock to Antigua in October 1782; master John Fish, from Greenock to Jamaica in December 1783.
[NAS.E504.15.27/28/30/33/36/38]

CHRISTY, master Andrew Lee, arrived in Annapolis, Maryland, in March 1775 from Port Glasgow.
[MdGaz#1541]

CLANSMAN, master John Snowdon, from Greenock *with passengers* to New Orleans in November 1824. [DPCA#1163]

CLARENDON OF GLASGOW, master John Denniston, from Greenock to Jamaica in January 1776.
[NAS.E504.15.26]

CLEMENTINA OF ARBROATH, 75 tons, master Alexander Stirling, arrived in Dundee from Virginia on 4 May 1734. [NAS.E70.1.2]

CLYDE OF GREENOCK, 70 tons, master John Shannon, from Greenock to Antigua on 21 March

1741, [CM#3276]; master John McCunn, arrived in Hampton, Virginia, on 4 August 1742 via Antigua. [PRO.CO5/1443]

CLYDE OF GLASGOW, master Robert Boyd, from Greenock via Madeira to Barbados in February 1749. [NAS.E504.15.4]

CLYDE, British built, master Duncan Montgomery, from Greenock to Jamaica in June 1782; master Robert Douglas, from Greenock to Grenada in October 1784; from Greenock to St Kitts in March 1786 . [NAS.E504.15.36/40/42]

CLYDE RIVER, master John White, from Greenock to St Kitts in December 1758, [NAS.E504.15.9]

COCHRANE, master Archibald Steel, from Port Glasgow to Virginia in December 1750. [NAS.E504.28/ 5]

COLLIN OF NORTH QUEENSFERRY, 70 tons, master James Brown, from Leith to St Kitts in November 1764. [NAS.E504.22.11]

COLUMBUS OF GREENOCK, master John Wilson, from Greenock to Jamaica in November 1784; from Greenock to Jamaica in November 1785. [NAS.E504.15.40/42]; master James Wilson, from Greenock *with passengers* to Savannah la Mar and Martha Brae, Jamaica, in December 1786. [GMerc: 12.1786]

COLUMBUS, 365 tons, Captain Bisset, from Dundee to Savannah, Georgia, in January 1827. [DPCA#1324]

COMMERCE, 'a new ship', master Robert Spears, from Greenock to Kingston, Morant Bay, Port Antonio, etc, Jamaica, in February 1787, *"Wanted for Jamaica, a house carpenter and a gardener"*. [GMerc:12.1786]

CONCORD OF GLASGOW, master James Butcher, arrived in Virginia on 29 March 1728 from Glasgow; arrived in Greenock on 8 October 1728 from Virginia. [EEC#500/554]; master James Butcher, arrived in Dundee on 18 July 1730 from Virginia; arrived in Dundee from Virginia on 19 July 1731; arrived in Dundee from Virginia on 19 September 1732; arrived in Arbroath from Virginia on 21 September 1733; arrived in Leith on 26 September 1734 from Virginia; arrived in Dundee in April 1735 from Virginia. [NAS,CE70.1.1/2][CM#2259]

CONCORD OF ARBROATH, 100 tons, British Built, master Patrick Spink, {died at sea}, to Virginia in 1740, returned to Arbroath on 24 November 1740 from Virginia under master John Spink, [NAS.CE53.1.3]; master David Fraser, arrived in Arbroath on 17 November 1741 from the York River, Virginia, [NAS.CE53.1.3]; from Dundee to Boston, New England, on 4 January 1743. [NAS.E504.11.1]; master John Fraser, arrived in Montrose on 7 December 1744 from Annapolis, Maryland. [NAS.E504.24.1]

CONCORD, master John Fraser, arrived in Annapolis, Maryland, from Montrose in August 1745. [MdGaz#16]

CONCORD, master James Watt, from Leith to Wilmington, North Carolina, 22 February 1772. [NAS.E504.22.17]

CONCORD, master Robert Workman, from Greenock *with passengers* to St Kitts and Antigua in July 1786. [GMerc][NAS.E504.15.43]

CONCORD, a 174 ton brig, master Robert Lithgow, from Dundee *with passengers* to New York in April 1816. [DPCA#715]

CONFIDENCE, a 150 ton brig, master John Wesley, from Dundee to New York in June 1828. [DPCA#1351]

CONSTABLE, a galley, master John Lyall, from Leith to Boston, New England, in October 1760. [NAS.E504.22.13]

CORNWALLIS OF GREENOCK, master Robert McKinlay, from Greenock to St Kitts in December 1779; master Francis House, from Greenock to Antigua in October 1783; from Greenock to Antigua in October 1784. [NAS.E504.15.32/38/40]; a brigantine, master Robert McKinlay, from Greenock *with passengers* bound for Antigua in December 1786. [GMerc:12.1786]

COUNTESS OF EGLINTON, master Robert Reid, from Greenock to Antigua in January 1776; from Greenock to Antigua in September 1776 [NAS.E504.15.26]

COUNTESS OF GALLOWAY, from Creetown *with passengers* bound for Kingston, Jamaica, on 15 March 1793. [DGA]

COURIER OF GREENOCK, master Alexander McLarty, from Greenock to Barbados in October 1786. [NAS.E504.15.43]

CRANSTON GALLEY OF CAPE FEAR, 120 tons, Plantation built, master Robert Johnston, from Kirkcaldy in April 1754 bound for Cape Fear, North Carolina; master William Bell, from Leith to Cape Fear in October 1755. [NAS.E504.20.3; E504.22.7]

CRAWFORD OF BOSTON, a 60 ton brigantine, master William Smith, arrived in Charleston, South Carolina, on 26 December 1752 from Glasgow via Gibraltar. [PRO.CO5.510]

CRAWFORD OF GLASGOW, 150 tons, master James McLean, from Leith to Maryland in September 1769. [NAS.E504.22.15]

CULLODEN, 159 tons, master P. Wallace, from Alloa via Leith *with passengers* bound for New York in March 1828. [S.XII.853]

CUMBERLAND, Captain Garioch, from Aberdeen bound for Antigua in 1747 when captured by the French and taken to Martinique. [SM.IX.506]

CUNNINGHAM, master Robert McLeish, from Irvine, Ayrshire, bound for New York in June 1761; from Irvine via Liverpool to New York in April 1762. [NAS.E504.18.5]

CUNNINGHAM, British built, master Theopilius Tyre, from Greenock to Dominica in December 1784; from Greenock to Dominica in November 1785. [NAS.E504.15.40/42]

CYGNET, a 150 ton brig, master John Henderson, from Dundee *with passengers* to New York in September 1815, also in May 1817. [DPCA#685/770]

DAEDELUS, Captain Scott, from Leith *with passengers* bound for Miramachi on 3 April 1828. [S.XII.852]

DALRYMPLE OF GLASGOW, master Robert Cobham, from Greenock to Virginia 17 February 1741. [CM#3262]

DAVID AND ANN OF LEITH, 150 ton, British built, master Alexander Ritchie, from Leith to New York in August 1773. [E504.22.18]; arrived in Philadelphia after a 4 month voyage from Fort George *with 250 passengers from Sutherland.* [Glasgow Chronicle:3.6.1774]

DELIGHT OF DUNDEE, master Alexander Ogilvie, from Dundee via Montrose, Angus, to the Potomac River, Virginia, in January 1751, and return to Montrose. [NAS.E504.11.2][NAS.RD211.2.107]

DENNISTOUN, master Patrick Carnegie, from Port Glasgow to Virginia in March 1752; from Greenock to the West Indies on 1 February 1755; from Greenock via Cork to the West Indies in September 1756. [NAS.E504.28.5][AJ#454/370]

DENNISTOUN OF BOSTON, a 90 ton snow, master Colin Campbell, arrived in Charleston, South Carolina, on 29 January 1759 from Glasgow; master Hugh Porter, arrived in Charleston on 29 November 1762 from Glasgow; arrived in Charleston on 28 February 1764 from Glasgow. [PRO.CO5.510/511]

DIAMOND, Captain Arthur, arrived in Dundee from Virginia on 6 December 1734. [NAS.CE70.1.2]

DIANA, a brig, master Thomas Calder, from Leith via Dundee *with passengers* to Halifax, and Pictou in March 1805. [DPCA#132]

DIANA, Captain McCulloch, from Greenock to Jamaica and Honduras on 28 March 1819. [EEC#18822]

DILIGENCE OF GLASGOW, at Greenock bound for Virginia in March 1728; master James Baillie, arrived in Greenock on 30 November from Norfolk, Virginia. [EEC#448/570]

DILIGENCE OF ABERDEEN, a brigantine, master George Duncan, arrived in Annapolis, Maryland, in May 1749 from Aberdeen. [MdGaz#214]; from Aberdeen to Antigua in March 1752. [AJ#220]

DILIGENCE, master Charles Robinson, arrived in Boston, New England, on15 November 1763 *with 91 passengers* from Scotland. [PAB]

DILIGENCE OF GREENOCK, 100 tons, master Charles Robinson, arrived in Charleston, South Carolina, on 25 April 1764 via St Kitts. [PRO.CO5.510]

DILIGENCE, master Peter Orr, from Greenock to
Barbados in November 1779. [NAS.E504.15.32]

DOLLY, William Morrison, from Leith to Cape Fear in
June 1757. [NAS.E504.22.7]

DOLPHIN OF DUNDEE, master John Glass, from
Dundee to Jamaica in 1753. [NAS.CE70.1.3]

DOLPHIN, a snow, master David Alexander, arrived in
Annapolis, Maryland, in May 1747, from Glasgow.
[MdGaz#110]

DOLPHIN OF CHARLESTON, a 60 ton brigantine,
master James Rea, arrived in Charleston, South
Carolina, on 24 February 1763 from Dundee;
arrived in Charleston on 21 November 1763 from
Dundee. [PRO.CO5.510]

DOLPHIN OF AYR, master Alexander McClure, from Ayr
to Newfoundland in February 1772; master Andrew
Burns, from Ayr to Newfoundland in March 1773.
[NAS.E504.4.5/6]

DOVE, master John Ratersby, from Greenock *with
passengers* bound for Boston, New England, in
August 1725. [EEC#32]

DOVE OF NEW ENGLAND, master James Taylor,
arrived in Greenock on 15 July 1728, from Boston,
New England; from Greenock to Boston 9
September 1728. [EEC#516/543]

DOVE, from Greenock via Madeira, Barbados, Antigua to
Virginia and return in 174-   [NAS.CS96/1920]

DOVE OF GLASGOW, master William Semple, from Port
Glasgow to Jamaica in September 1743; from
Greenock to Jamaica in December 1746; from
Greenock via Cork to St Kitts in December 1747;
from Greenock via Cork to St Kitts 9 January 1748.
[NAS.E504.28.1;15.3][CM#4252]

DREGHORN, Captain Kelburn, from Greenock to Jamaica on 3 January 1757. [AJ#470]

DRUMMOND OF GLASGOW, master James Spiers, from Greenock bound for Philadelphia, the Chesapeake, and Barbados in 1719, [NAS.AC7.27.2186]; master John Thomson, from Greenock bound for Virginia on 21 January 1728; arrived in Greenock on 8 October 1728 from Virginia. [EEC#420/554]

DUCHESS OF GLOUCESTER, 205 tons, master John King, from Glasgow *with passengers* bound for New York in October 1823. *'beds and bedding furnished by the owners'.* [DPCA#1097]

DUCHESS OF LENNOX OF GREENOCK, master Dougal McLellan, from Greenock to Grenada in June 1776. [NAS.E504.15.26]

DUKE OF ARGYLE, master William King, from Port Glasgow to Virginia in June 1752. [NAS.E504.28/5]

DUKE OF CUMBERLAND OF GLASGOW, master Hugh Brown, from Port Glasgow to Virginia in March 1748; master James Dunlop, from Port Glasgow to Virginia in March 1751, and in March 1752. [NAS.E504.28.4/5]

DUNLOP OF GLASGOW, a sloop, master David Alexander, from Glasgow in December 1747, arrived in Annapolis, Maryland, in February 1748, [MdGaz#145]; from Port Glasgow to Virginia in August 1748, to South Carolina in October 1751. [NAS.E504.28/3/4/5]; arrived in Annapolis in August 1754 from Glasgow, from Annapolis bound for Glasgow in October 1754, [MdGaz#383/492]

DUNLOP OF BOSTON, 120 ton snow, master Ralph Boyle, arrived in Charleston, South Carolina, during November 1759 from Glasgow. [PRO.CO5.510]

DUNMUIR, master James Ewing, from the Chesapeake to Glasgow in October 1761. [MdGaz#858]

DUNTREATH OF LEITH, 150 tons, master James Edmondstone, from Leith to Grenada in April 1776. [NAS.E504.22.20]

EAGLE OF NEW YORK, a 90 ton snow, at Lochcraigneish in Argyll, having been brought there by pirates in February 1720, offered for sale in June 1724. [EEC#401]

EAGLE, Captain Blaine, arrived in New York in September 1784 from Glasgow. [MdGaz#1966]

EARL OF GLASGOW, master John Boyle, from Greenock to Jamaica and Tobago in April 1778; from Greenock to Grenada in March 1779. [NAS.E504.15.29/30/31]

EDDYSTONE, master Thomas Ramsay, from Gravesend via Orkney to Eastmain, Moose, Hudson's Bay, and return in 1807, 1808, 1810, 1811, 1812, 1813, 1814, and 1816; master John Davidson, from Gravesend via Orkney to Moose, Hudson's Bay, in 1817; master Benjamin Bell, from Gravesend via Orkney to Moose, York Factory, and return in 1818, 1819, 1820, 1821, 1822, and 1823. [HBCA#SM23/24/25/26]

EDINBURGH, master James Russell, at Annapolis, Maryland, in December 1747. [MdGaz#141]

EDINBURGH, 300 tons, master Ninian Bryce, from Leith to Jamaica in 1748, returned to Leith on 21 December 1749. [SM.XI.602]

EDINBURGH, 140 tons, master John Lyon, arrived in Charleston, South Carolina, on 29 December 1752 via Jamaica. [PRO.CO5.510]

EDINBURGH OF GREENOCK, 100 tons, master Robert Ramsay, from Greenock to St Christopher's in

March 1746, [NAS.E504.15.2]; master Walter Duncan, arrived in Charleston, South Carolina, on 22 April 1758; master Alexander Ritchie, arrived in Charleston on 3 December 1759 from Kirkcaldy; arrived in Charleston on 24 December 1760 via Tenneriffe. [PRO.CO5.510]

EDINBURGH OF LEITH, a 120 ton snow, master Thomas Murray, from Leith to Jamaica in November 1758, [NAS.E504.22.8]; master John Grant, from Leith to Philadelphia and Monte Cristo, Boyds Hole, Virginia (?) 1761/1762. [NAS.GD237.8.4]; master Thomas Murray, from Leith to Jamaica in May 1760; master James Hamilton, from Leith to Jamaica in January 1762; from Leith to Jamaica in May 1763, [NAS.E504.22.9/10]

EDINBURGH, a brig, from Campbeltown, Argyll, *with 120 passengers* bound for North Carolina in 1770; from Campbeltown *with 100 passengers* bound for the Island of St John's in the Bay of St Lawrence, 1771. [NAS.RH1.2.933/ii]

EDINBURGH PACKET, from Leith *with passengers* to New York, arrived there in 1798. [EWJ#25]

EDWARD AND ANN, from Gravesend via Orkney and the Isle of Lewis to York Factory, Hudson Bay, and return in 1811. [HBCA#2M27]

EGLINTON, master George Buchanan, from Greenock to Guadaloupe in November 1759. [NAS.E504.15.9]

ELDERSLIE, master James Scott, from Greenock to Jamaica in February 1781. [NAS.E504.15.33]

ELIZA OF LONDON, 65 tons, master John Miln, from Aberdeen to Maryland in May 1743. [NAS.E504.1.1]

ELIZA, master George Hynd, from Dundee to New York on 1 April 1827; from Dundee *with passengers* to

New York on 11 October 1827; from Dundee to
New York on 28 May 1828.
[DPCA#1288/1313/1348]

ELIZABETH OF MONTROSE, master David Gentleman,
from Montrose to Jamaica by 1719. [NAS.AC9.647]

ELIZABETH OF GLASGOW, master Thomas Buchanan,
from Greenock on 19 December 1728 bound for
Virginia. [EEC#579]

ELIZABETH, a brig, master Daniel Clark, arrived in
Charleston, South Carolina, on 11 December 1740
from Glasgow. [SCGaz#356]

ELIZABETH OF VIRGINIA, master Alexander Leslie,
arrived in Montrose on 29 August 1748 from the
Rappahannock River, Virginia. [NAS.E504.24.1]

ELIZABETH, a snow, master James Parks, arrived in
Annapolis, Maryland, in March 1747 from
Aberdeen. [MdGaz#101]

ELIZABETH, Captain Weir, from Greenock to Antigua in
January 1756; Captain Dick, from Greenock to
Barbados in December 1756. [AJ#418/466]

ELIZABETH OF GREENOCK, master William Orr, from
Greenock to Jamaica in October 1744; master
James Park, from Greenock to Antigua in March
1777. [NAS.E504.15.2/27]

ELIZABETH OF GLASGOW, 120 ton ship, master
Alexander Keir, in Charleston, South Carolina,
during February 1767. [PRO.CO5.511]

ELIZABETH OF BO'NESS, 100 tons, master Hercules
Angus, arrived in Charleston, South Carolina, on 18
November 1764 from Bo'ness, West Lothian;
arrived in Charleston on 7 November 1766 from
Bo'ness. [PRO.CO5.511]

ELIZABETH, master James Scott, from Greenock to Jamaica in February 1778; from Greenock to Jamaica in December 1779; master John Fish, from Greenock to Jamaica in December 1785. [NAS.E504.15.29/32/42]; master John Fish, from Greenock bound for Montago Bay, Lucea, and Green Island, Jamaica, in December 1786, *"Wanted for Jamaica, a carpenter"*. [GMerc:12.1786]

ELIZABETH, master John Paterson, from Port Glasgow to Virginia in June 1784; master James Paterson, from Port Glasgow to Virginia in July 1784. [NAS.E504.28.37]

ELIZABETH, master Andrew Grierson, from Port Glasgow *with passengers* to New Orleans in August 1827. [DPCA#1305]

ELIZABETH AND MARY OF DUNDEE, a 223 ton brig, master Henry Walker, from Port Glasgow *with passengers* to New York in December 1827. [DPCA#1319]

EMERALD, a brig, master Benjamin Bell, from Gravesend via Orkney to Moose and Charlton Island, Hudson Bay, and return in 1817. [HBCA#2M27]

EMPEROR ALEXANDER, a brig, master Alexander Watt, from Aberdeen via Dundee *with passengers* to Charleston, South Carolina, in December 1815. [DPCA#693]

ENDEAVOUR OF WHITEHAVEN, master Isaac Binsley, from Greenock to Virginia on 13 January 1728; arrived in Greenock on 15 November 1728 from Virginia. [EEC#408/565]

ENDEAVOUR, master John Simpson, from Glasgow, was in October 1748 captured by a Spanish privateer off the Capes of Virginia. [MdGaz#185]

ENDEAVOUR, Captain Smith, from Greenock to Jamaica on 5 August 1749. [AJ#85]

ENDEAVOUR, master Robert Hamilton, from Glasgow via Dieppe, arrived in Annapolis, Maryland, in September 1749. [MdGaz#230]

ENTERPRISE, Captain Sheal, from the Clyde to Grenada in April 1798. [EWJ#15]

ERSKINE OF ALLOA, master James Miller, from Alloa to Virginia on 8 November 1773. [NAS.E504.2.6]

ESTHER, a brigantine, master Robert Johnston, from Savannah, Georgia, to Kirkcudbright on 24 April 1770. [GaGaz#2.5.1770]

EUPHEMIA OF PORT GLASGOW, 70 tons, master Jonathan Bowman, from Glasgow in June 1725 bound for Barbados, arrived in the Rappahannock River, Virginia, on 7 December 1725; master James Cochrane, captured off the Capes of Virginia on 10 September 1727 by the Spanish. [EEC#420]

EUPHEMIA OF GLASGOW, 70 ton pink, master John Lyon, arrived in Charleston, South Carolina, on 18 March 1732, from Charleston to Cape Fear, North Carolina, 16 April 1732. [PRO.CO5.509]

EUPHRATES OF GLASGOW, master John Campbell, from Greenock to Jamaica in December 1783; from Greenock to Jamaica in December 1784; from Greenock to Jamaica in December 1785. [NAS.E504.15.38/40/42]; from Greenock bound for Montago Bay, Lucea, Green Island, Savannah la Mar, and Black River, Jamaica, in December 1786, *"Wanted for Jamaica, a carpenter who must be well acquainted with the wheelwright and pump boring business"*.[GMerc:12.1786]

EUSTON, master John McKeay, from Port Glasgow to Boston, New England, in November 1742. [NAS.E504.28.1]

EXPEDITION OF GLASGOW, 80 tons, master William Dunlop, arrived in Charleston, South Carolina, in 1716 from Glasgow. [PRO.CO5/508]

EXPEDITION OF INVERKEITHING, 150 tons, master David Ingles, from Leith to Grenada in May 1765. [NAS.E504.22.12]

EXPEDITION, a brig, master George Watson, from Aberdeen to Jamaica on 19 October 1820; from Aberdeen *with passengers* bound via Madeira to Montego Bay, Jamaica, in November 1825. [MC#50][DPCA#1215]

FAIR PENITENT OF GREENOCK, Plantation built, master John Hunter, from Greenock to Barbados in February 1785; from Greenock to Barbados in November 1785; from Greenock to Barbados in June 1786. [NAS.E504.15.40/42/43]; master John Hunter, from Greenock *with passengers* bound for Barbados in January 1787. [GMerc.12.1786]

FAME OF DUNDEE, 186 tons, master William Thornton, arrived in Charleston, South Carolina, on 27 February 1767 via Madeira and the Canary Islands. [PRO.CO5.511]

FAME OF GREENOCK, master James Fyffe, from Greenock to St Kitts in November 1779. [NAS.E504.15.32]

FAME OF AYR, master James Taylor, from Ayr to Virginia in September 1785. [NAS.E504.4.8]

FAME, Captain Frew, from Greenock to Jamaica on 25 February 1819. [EEC#16808]

FANNY OF BOSTON, 160 tons, master Archibald
Galbraith, arrived in Charleston, South Carolina, on
20 December 1766 from Glasgow. [PRO.CO5.511]

FANNY OF PORT GLASGOW, master William McKie,
from Greenock to Antigua in May 1776.
[NAS.E504.15.26]

FANNY OF GLASGOW, master John Campbell, from
Greenock to Jamaica in December 1778; from
Greenock to Jamaica in December 1779; master
Robert Wilson, from Greenock to Jamaica in
January 1782; master James Young, from
Greenock to Antigua in October 1782; from
Greenock to Antigua in October 1783.
[NAS.E504.15.30/32/35/37/38]

FANNY, master William Leslie, from Dundee to Antigua
in May 1787. [DCA: H3796]

FANNY, a brigantine, master George Henderson, from
Greenock *with passengers* bound for Cape Fear,
North Carolina, in January 1787. [GMerc.12.1786]

FELLOWSHIP HALL, (formerly the Mary Bedward),
master James Noble, from Port Glasgow bound for
Kingston, Jamaica, in January 1787, *"good
accommodation for passengers"*.
[GMerc:12.1786]

FINDLAY, master James Fairrie, from Port Glasgow to
Jamaica in December 1783. [NAS.E504.28.36]

FISHER AND FRIENDSHIP, William Forrester, from
Leith to Georgia 4 February 1772.
[NAS.E504.22.17]

FLORA, master William Cochrane, from Greenock to
Antigua in November 1779. [NAS.E504.15.32];
master John Rankine, from Port Glasgow to
Charlestown, South Carolina, in November 1783.
[NAS.E504.22.36]; 250 tons, master Archibald

Henry, from Port Glasgow *with passengers* bound for Quebec in March 1787. [GMerc:12.1786]

FORTH OF LEITH, 120 tons, master John Brown, from Leith to Virginia in May 1756. [NAS.E504.22.7]

FORTITUDE, master David Johnston, from Greenock to Jamaica in April 1781; master Thomas Mitchell, from Greenock to Jamaica in January 1783; from Greenock to St Kitts in December 1783; from Greenock to St Kitts in March 1785 [NAS.E504.15.33/37/38/40]; master David Hunter, from Greenock to Grenada in December 1786, *"Wanted for the West Indies. Two good house carpenters, one of them to understand making cartwheels, a blacksmith, a millwright, and a wheelwright".* [GMerc.12.1786]

FORTUNE OF GLASGOW, master Robert Arthur, from Port Glasgow to Antigua in 1716. [NAS.AC9.584]

FORTUNE OF GLASGOW, master James McBrayer, from Greenock to Virginia in March 1728. [EEC#431]

FORTUNE, master Archibald Bogg, from Greenock to Grenada in November 1784; master Robert Hunter, from Greenock to Tortola in October 1785. [NAS.E504.15.40/41]

FORTUNE, a brig, Captain Craig, from Dundee *with passengers* to Charleston, South Carolina, in March 1816. [DPCA#702]

FOUNDLING, Captain Hardie, from Greenock to St Vincent on 4 June 1819. [EEC#16851]

FRAU VAN KALCREUTH OF MEMEL, master Peter Smith, from Greenock to St Thomas, Danish West Indies, in November 1782. [NAS.E504.15.37]

FRIENDS, master Thomas Choate, from Greenock *with friends* to New York on 10 November 1824. [DPCA#1154]

FRIENDSHIP OF BOSTON, master Henry Hill, arrived in Leith in July 1696 from Boston, New England, possibly bound for Rotterdam. [NAS.GD1.885/23]

FRIENDSHIP OF LEITH, master Walter Fleeth, arrived in the Lower James River, Virginia, on 10 January 1716, from Scotland. [PRO.CO5.1443]

FRIENDSHIP OF WHITEHAVEN, master Isaac Langton, arrived in Greenock on 18 July 1722 from Virginia. [EEC#565]

FRIENDSHIP OF MONTROSE, master John Buchanan, arrived in Montrose on 30 November 1741 from the Rappahannock River, Virginia. [NAS.CE53.1.3]; master Alexander Beattie, arrived in Montrose on 31 December 1742 from the Rappahannock River, Virginia. [NAS.E504.24.1]

FRIENDSHIP, master James Lyon, from Greenock via Cork to St Kitts and Jamaica on 24 April 1756. [AJ#434][NAS.E504.15.7]

FRIENDSHIP OF BO'NESS, 241 tons, master William Miller, arrived in Charleston, South Carolina, during October 1760 from Bo'ness; master Hercules Angus, arrived in Charleston on 27 January 1761 via Amsterdam; in Charleston in January 1764. [PRO.CO5.510/511]

FRIENDSHIP OF AYR, master John Smith, from Ayr to Antigua in March 1774. [NAS.E504.4.6]

FRIENDSHIP OF PHILADELPHIA, 120 ton Plantation built, master Thomas Jann, from Leith to Philadelphia 6 May 1775. [NAS.E504.22.19]

FRIENDSHIP OF CELLARDYKE, 100 tons, master Andrew Reid, from Leith to Grenada in December 1775. [NAS.E504.22.20]

FRIENDSHIP OF GREENOCK, master James Kerr, from Greenock to Antigua in May 1776. [NAS.E504.15.26]; master Duncan McRob, from the Clyde *with passengers* bound for Antigua on 18 November 1782, storm-damaged, captured by the American privateer The Commander on 24 January 1783, liberated by the Royal Navy and taken to Antigua, landed on 29 January 1783. [NAS.AC7.61]

FRIENDSHIP OF LEITH, 150 tons, British built, master George Ritchie, from Leith to Hampton, Virginia, in May 1784. [NAS.E504.22.28]

FRIENDSHIP, master Alexander Wilson, from Greenock to Jamaica in December 1778; master Adam Coursar, from Greenock to Jamaica in June 1786. [NAS.E504.15.30/43]

FRIENDSHIP, master William Service, from Greenock to Barbados and St Lucia in November 1779; master Alexander Wylie, from Greenock to St Lucia in November 1781; master Duncan McRobb, from Greenock to Antigua in October 1782. [NAS.E504.15.32/35/37]

FRIENDSHIP, master Paul White, from Port Glasgow to Port Roseway, Nova Scotia, in April 1785. [NAS.E504.22.39]

FRISKY, master George Leitch, from Greenock to St Lucia in November 1782. [NAS.E504.15.37]

FUNCHALL, Captain Crews, from Greenock to Newfoundland on 20 March 1819. [EEC#16819]

GALEN, a sloop, master H. Herriman, arrived in Belfast, USA, from Scotland in 1820. [PAB]

GENERAL DALLING, master Robert Spears, from Greenock to Jamaica in March 1779; master John Hartwell, from Greenock to Jamaica in November 1781. [NAS.E504.15.30/35]

GEORGE OF GLASGOW, a galley, master David Buckling, arrived in the Potomac River, Virginia, before 1718, via Barbados. [PRO.CO5.1320]

GEORGE OF GREENOCK, master John Stewart, from Greenock via Cork to Barbados 29 December 1727; arrived in Greenock on 12 September 1728 from St Kitts. [EEC#405/543]

GEORGE, Captain Crawford, arrived in the Rappahannock around 20 October 1745 from Glasgow

GEORGE OF LEITH, 180 ton Plantation built, master Alexander Alexander, from Leith to Charleston, South Carolina, in September 1773. [E504.22.18]

GEORGE, a 170 ton brig, Captain Reid, from Dundee *with passengers* to Charleston, South Carolina, in July 1816. [DPCA#729]

GIRZIE OF GREENOCK, master John Johnson, from Port Glasgow to Virginia in July 1750; master Henry White, from Port Glasgow to Virginia in April 1751; to Virginia in November 1751, to Virginia in August 1752; master John Sproat, from Greenock to Antigua in October 1774. [NAS.E504.28.4/5; E504.15.24]

GLASFORD OF CHARLESTON, 150 tons, master Robert Hall, arrived in Charleston, South Carolina, on 14 April 1759 from Glasgow. [PRO.CO5.510]

GLASGOW PACKET OF GREENOCK, master Thomas Watson, from Greenock to Barbados on 12 December 1741. [CM#3318]

GLASGOW, master James Coats, from Greenock to Antigua in November 1758; master William Cunningham, from Greenock to Jamaica in November 1765. [NAS.E504.15.9/13]; master John Dunn, arrived in Boston, New England, on 19 November 1767 *with passengers* from Glasgow; arrived in Boston on 28 May 1768 *with passengers* from Glasgow; arrived in Boston on 28 November 1768 *with passengers* from Glasgow; arrived in Boston on 1 June 1769 *with passengers* from Glasgow. [PAB]

GLASGOW, master Alexander Thomson, from Greenock to Barbados in November 1779; master Abraham Russell, from Greenock to Jamaica in October 1781; master John Blain, from Greenock to Barbados in April 1782; master Hugh Ferry, from Port Glasgow to Maryland in June 1785; master John Bowie, from Greenock to Jamaica in October 1786. [NAS.E504.15.32/34/35/42] [NAS.E504.22.39]

GLASGOW OF DUNDEE, a 164 ton brig, master Robert Kidd, from Dundee *with passengers* to Quebec in March 1815; master William Young [Captain Caithness?], from Dundee *with passengers* to St Andrews, New Brunswick, in February 1817. [DPCA#655/755]

GLENCAIRN, master James Glasgow, from Greenock to Jamaica 5 December 1747, [CM#4237]; from Greenock to St Kitts in November 1748; from Port Glasgow to Virginia in August 1752 [AJ#48][NAS.E504.28.5]

GOWAN, a 144 ton brig, master James Webster, from Dundee *with passengers* to New York in November 1816. [DPCA#740]

GRAHAM OF GLASGOW, master Patrick Jack, from Greenock to Virginia on 22 February 1728. [EEC#438]

GRAEMIE OF GLASGOW, master George Hunter, from Port Glasgow to Virginia in April 1751. [NAS.E504.28.4/5]

GRAND TURK OF GREENOCK, Captain Wyllie, from Greenock to Barbados in January 1750, [AJ#107]; master Robert Watson, from Greenock via the Canaries, and Madeira to Barbados in November 1750. [NAS.E504.15.4]

GRANGE OF GREENOCK, master Robert Jack, from Greenock to Barbados in October 1779; master William Kinnear, from Port Glasgow to Virginia in July 1783; master Robert Kerr, from Port Glasgow to Virginia in January 1785. [NAS.E504.15.31][NAS.E504.28.36/38]

GRANDVALE, master Robert Bain, from Greenock to Jamaica in February 1783; from Port Glasgow via Greenock to Jamaica in March 1784, also in November 1784. [NAS.E504.15.37/38]; master Robert Baine, from Port Glasgow to Kingston, Black River, and Savannah la Mar, Jamaica in January 1787 *"excellent accommodation for passengers"* [GMerc.12.1786]

GRATITUDE, a 150 ton brig, Captain Kinneir, from Dundee *with passengers* to New York in April 1817; master John Gellatly, from Dundee *with passengers* bound for Quebec and Montreal in June 1824; from Dundee *with passengers* bound for Quebec and Montreal in March 1825; from Dundee *with passengers* bound for Montreal in September 1825; from Dundee *with passengers* bound for Quebec and Montreal on 30 March 1827, landed at Quebec on 4 May 1827; from Dundee *with passengers* to Quebec and Montreal on 8 August 1827; master John Young, from Dundee to New York on 8 April 1828. [DPCA#770/1137/1173/1203/1285/1304/1339/1343]

GREENOCK MERCHANT OF GREENOCK, master James Crawford, arrived in Greenock on 31 March 1721 from Virginia. [EEC#365]

GREENOCK OF GLASGOW, master John Esdale, from Greenock to Virginia in March 1728; arrived in Greenock on 15 November 1728 from Virginia. [EEC#431/565]

GREENOCK, a snow, Captain Hill, from Greenock to Jamaica on 22 December 1753; master David Alexander, arrived in Annapolis in July 1755 from Glasgow; from Annapolis bound for Glasgow in October 1755. [AJ#312] [MdGaz#534/547]

GREENOCK OF GREENOCK, master Archibald McLarty, from Greenock to Jamaica in 27 March 1779. [NAS.E504.15.30][AJ#1627]

GRENADA, Captain Gilkison, from Greenock to Grenada on 19 January 1819. [EEC#16796]

HADLOW, master John Davidson, from Gravesend via Orkney to York Factory, Moose and Strutton Sound, Hudson's Bay, and return in 1816. [HBCA#2M31]

HALL, Captain McMillan, from Greenock to Jamaica on 4 January 1752. [AJ#211]

HAMILTON OF RENFREW, master John Scott, from Port Glasgow to Jamaica in February 1743. [NAS.E504.28.1]

HAMLET, Captain Clark, from Greenock to St Thomas and Tortula, Virgin Islands, on 3 March 1819. [EEC#16811]

HANNAH OF ROTTERDAM, Captain Wilson, from Rotterdam via Leith *with 300 Palatines* bound for Philadelphia, at Leith on 19 June 1746. [CM#4008]

HANNAH OF GREENOCK, a snow, master James Crawford, arrived in Savanna, Georgia, on 11 October 1766 via Jamaica, [PRO.CO5.710] [GaGaz]; master John McNachtane, from Greenock to Barbados in July 1776; master Thomas Wilkie from Greenock to Jamaica in November 1777. [NAS.E504.15.26/28][NAS.AC9.3182]

HANOVER, at Stranraer in February 1716, when bound from Belfast to the West Indies. [GCo]

HANOVER OF GLASGOW, a brigantine, master Garrett Garretts, from Glasgow to Guinea and St Kitts in 1719. [NAS.AC9/1042]

HANOVER, master Robert Pollock, from Greenock to Jamaica in January 1777. [NAS.E504.15.27]

HAPPY RETURN, master George Duncan, from (Leith?), Scotland, on 28 September 1698 via Dover, England, *with passengers* bound for Barbados, arrived there on 11 December 1698, returned to Scotland via Newfoundland in 1699. [NAS.RH15.101.3]

HARMONY, a barque, master John Young, from Leith *with passengers* bound for Quebec on 5 April 1828. [S.XII.846]

HARRIOT, 200 tons, master Thomas Herdman, from Aberdeen *with passengers* to Madeira, Barbados, Antigua and Virginia in 1768. [AJ#1044]

HARVEY, a brigantine, master Henry Ninian, arrived in Savannah, Georgia, on 5 March 1768 from Glasgow. [GaGaz: 9.3.1768]

HAWK, master Richard Hill, from Greenock via Cork to Jamaica and the West Indies in February 1755; Captain Campbell, from Greenock to Jamaica in January 1757; from Greenock to Jamaica in December 1758. [NAS.E504.15.7][AJ#474/575]

HEART OF OAK, master James Booth, from Dundee *with passengers* to Quebec in July 1827. [DPCA#1301]

HEBE, Captain Montgomery, from the Clyde to Newfoundland in April 1798. [EWJ#15]

HECTOR OF GREENOCK, master Richard Tucker, from Greenock to Tobago in January 1774. [NAS.E504.15.24]

HECTOR OF DUNDEE, master George Keay, from Dundee to New York in 1801. [NAS.CE70.1.9/57]

HECTOR OF DUNDEE, a 190 ton brigantine, master Andrew How, from Dundee *with passengers* to Quebec in March 1808, [DPCA#289]; master James Webster, from Dundee *with passengers* to Miramachi, New Brunswick, in 1816, also in March 1817. [DPCA#710/761/768]

HELEN OF LEITH, a 45 ton snow, master James Seaman, arrived in Charleston, South Carolina, on 14 October 1734 from Leith via London. [PRO.CO5.509]; returned to Leith in April 1735 from Georgia. [CM#2345]

HELEN, master Donald Edie, arrived in Charleston, South Carolina, in January 1757 from Leith. [SCGaz#1178]

HELEN, a brig, from Campbeltown *with 84 male and 60 female passengers* bound for North Carolina in 1769. [NAS.RH1.2.933/ii]

HELEN, a 185 ton brig, Captain Moore, from Dundee *with passengers* to Charleston, South Carolina, in December 1816. [DPCA#740/747]

HELEN, a brig, master Thomas Erskine, from Dundee *with passengers* bound for Canada, shipwrecked off Rockall in 1824. [DPCA]

HELENA OF BOSTON, master William Davis, from Kirkwall, Orkney, to Boston, New England, 1 September 1749, also 23 May 1750, 8 April 1751. [NAS.E504.26.2]

HELENA, master Daniel Crawford, from Greenock to St Kitts in October 1784. [NAS.E504.15.40]

HENRY, Captain Atkinson, from Dundee to Richibucto on 21 May 1825. [DPCA#1191]

HERALD, a 305 ton barque, master James Goldie, from Dundee *with passengers* bound for Charleston and Savannah in September 1827; from Dundee to Savannah in August 1828. [DPCA#1304/1355]

HERCULES OF MONTROSE, master Alexander Gordon, from Scotland to Barbados in 1716. [NAS.E508.10.6]

HERCULES OF AYR, master John McGowan, from Ayr to Newfoundland in May 1769; master William Thomson, from Ayr to Antigua in February 1776. [NAS.E504.4.5/6].

HERCULES, master Moses Cadenhead, from Aberdeen *with passengers* to Grenada, Dominica, Tobago, Barbados and Jamaica in January 1775. [AJ#1400]

HERCULES OF DUNDEE, a 151 ton brig, from Dundee *with passengers* to Quebec in March 1816. [DPCA#702]

HERCULES, a 252 ton barque, Captain Birnie, from Dundee *with passengers* to Savannah and New Orleans on 11 January 1828. [DPCA#1321/1327]

HERO OF AYR, master John Bowie, from Ayr to Antigua and Montserrat in February 1769, in November 1769 and also in February 1771. [NAS.E504.4.5]

HERO OF GLASGOW, master David Scott, from Greenock to Jamaica in January 1770; master John

Morrice, from Greenock to St Lucia in October 1779; master John Rankine, from Greenock to Antigua in January 1782; master Thomas Falcon, from Greenock to St Kitts in March 1785. [NAS.E504.15.18/32/35/40]

HOME, British built, master John Paterson, from Greenock to Grenada in November 1785; from Greenock to Grenada in August 1786. [NAS.E504.15.42/43]

HOMER, a snow, Captain Robert Christie, from Glasgow to the James River, Virginia, in 1769. [MdGaz#1229]

HOPE, Captain Nicholls, from Scotland bound for the West Indies in 1747 when captured by the French and taken to Bilbao. [SM.IX.506]

HOPE, master Alexander Murray, from Leith to Annapolis, Maryland, in October 1757. [NAS.E504.22.6]

HOPE OF IRVINE, master Matthew Brown, from Campbeltown via Cork to St Kitts in December 1775. [NAS.E504.8.5]

HOPE OF GREENOCK, master Archibald Thomson, from Greenock to Jamaica in January 1779. [NAS.E504.15.30]

HOPE, master Robert Steel, from Greenock to Tortola, the Virgin Islands, in December 1779; master George Conn, from Greenock to Tortula in January 1782; from Greenock to Tortula in January 1783. [NAS.E504.15.32/35/37]

HOPE, master John Clouston, from Port Glasgow to Boston, New England, in October 1783; master Archibald Henry, from Port Glasgow to Newfoundland in July 1784; master John Montgomerie, from Port Glasgow to Tortula, the

Virgin Islands, in November 1785.
[NAS.E504.22.36/37/40]

HOPE, British built, master John Barbour, from Greenock
to Grenada in June 1785; from Greenock to St Kitts
in November 1785; from Greenock **with
passengers** to Grenada in June 1786. [GMerc]
[NAS.E504.15.41/42/43]

HOPE, master Edward Kerr, from Greenock to
Newfoundland in June 1785. [NAS.E504.22.39]

HOPE, Captain Newman, from Greenock to St Thomas,
in the Virgin Islands, 23 June 1821. [EEC#17172]

HOUSTON, master Robert Chisholm, from Greenock to
St Kitts in January 1765; master John Simpson,
from Greenock to St Kitts in January 1767.
[NAS.E504.15.12/13]

HUDSON'S BAY, master Joseph Spurrell, from
Gravesend via Orkney to Churchill, Hudson's Bay,
and return in 1751; master William Norton, from
Gravesend via Orkney to Richmond Fort, Hudson's
Bay, and return in 1752, 1753, 1754, 1755, 1756;
master Jonathon Fowler, from Gravesend via
Orkney to Albany, Hudson's Bay, in 1751; from
Gravesend via Orkney to Richmond Fort, Hudson's
Bay, and return in 1759. [HBCA#2M31/32/121]

HUME, master Duncan McLean, from Port Glasgow to
Jamaica in February 1775. [NAS.E504.28.24]

HUMILITY, Captain Jack, from Greenock to South
Carolina on 27 December 1746. [CM#4092]

HUNTER, master Abram Hunter, from Greenock to
Jamaica in February 1778; master John Service,
from Greenock to Jamaica in November 1778.
[NAS.E504.15.29/30]

HUNTER, master John Kinneir, from Port Glasgow via Cork to Quebec in February 1786. [NAS.E504.28.40]

HUNTER, Captain Lusk, from the Clyde to Halifax, Nova Scotia, in August 1798. [EWJ#34]

HUNTER OF ABERDEEN, master James Logan, from Aberdeen *with 5 passengers* bound for Halifax, Nova Scotia, in May 1817. [NAS.E504.1.27]

HYNDMAN, master James Lyon, from Greenock to St Kitts in May 1755. [AJ#382][NAS.E504.15.7]

IMMACULATE CONCEPTION OF NAPLES, master Paula Balsamo, from Greenock to St Thomas, Danish West Indies, in January 1783. [NAS.E504.15.37]

INDEPENDENCE, master Alexander Osburne, from Port Glasgow to Philadelphia in August 1783. [NAS.E504.22.36]

INDEPENDENCE, from Dundee *with passengers* to New York in August 1816. [DPCA#729]

INDIAN QUEEN OF ABERDEEN, master John Ferguson, arrived in Aberdeen on 27 May 1743 from Virginia. [NAS.E504.1.1]

INDIAN QUEEN OF DUMFRIES, from Kirkcudbright to Virginia and return in 1748-1749. [NAS.RD4.1752.2, charter party]

INDUSTRY OF GLASGOW, master Adam Chisholm, from Greenock to St Kitts on 30 April 1741. [CM#3292]

INDUSTRY OF BERWICK, a 82 ton brigantine, master David Deas, arrived in Charleston, South Carolina, on 13 April 1764. [PRO.CO5.511]

INDUSTRY OF ABERDEEN, Captain Ross, from Aberdeen to Antigua in March 1752. [AJ#222]

INDUSTRY OF GREENOCK, master James Warden, from Greenock to St Kitts in January 1752; from Glasgow to Antigua in February 1753, from Greenock to Barbados on 1 December 1753; from Greenock via Cork to St Kitts in February 1755; from Glasgow to Antigua in March 1756. [AJ#267/309/425][NAS.E504.15.7/9]

INDUSTRY OF LEITH, 100 tons, master Andrew Cowan, arrived in Charleston, South Carolina, on 25 January 1753 from Leith. [PRO.CO5.510]

INDUSTRY OF BO'NESS, 100 tons, master William Muir, arrived in Charleston, South Carolina, on 27 January 1759 from Glasgow; master Hercules Angus, arrived in Charleston on 31 January 1760 from Bo'ness. [PRO.CO5.510]

INDUSTRY OF BERWICK, an 82 ton brigantine, master David Deas, arrived in Charleston, South Carolina, on 13 April 1764 via Bristol. [PRO.CO5.511]

ISABEL OF ARBROATH, master David Ogilvie, from Arbroath in April 1742 bound for Boston, New England. [NAS.CE53.1.3]

ISABELLA OF GREENOCK, master Abraham Hastie, arrived in the Potomac River, Virginia, via Barbados before 1718. [PRO.CO5.CO5.1320]

ISABELLA, master William Hodyart, from Greenock to Grenada in October 1765; Captain Chisholm, from Greenock to St Kitts in February 1758; from Greenock to St Kitts in December 1758. [NAS.E504.15.13] [AJ#529/573]

ISABELLA OF GREENOCK, master William McLennan, from Greenock *with 27 passengers* bound for Jamaica in July 1775. [PRO.T47/12]; master Hugh

Hendry, from Greenock to St Kitts in March 1778. [NAS.E504.15.29]

ISABELLA, master Jonathan Taylor, from Port Glasgow to Virginia in August 1784; master John McAllister, from Port Glasgow to Virginia in February 1785. [NAS.E504.28.37/38]

ISABELLA, Captain Cameron, from Greenock to Jamaica on 30 January 1819; Captain Patton, from Greenock to Montego Bay, Jamaica, on 26 April 1819. [EEC#16797/16834]

ISABELLA, Captain Thomson, from Aberdeen to Pictou, Nova Scotia, on 15 June 1820. [MC#32]

ISABELLA, a 300 ton brig, master Thomas Fyfe, from Dundee *with passengers* to New York on 10 April 1826. [DPCA#1236]

ISABELLA SIMPSON, 307 tons, Captain Young, from Leith to Jamaica in February 1817, [S#3]; Captain Fraser, from Leith *with passengers* to St George's and St Mary's, Jamaica, on 15 September 1821. [EEC#17190]; Captain Mure, from Dundee *with passengers* via Madeira to Jamaica in March 1824. [DPCA#1123]

ISBELL OF GREENOCK, master John Park, arrived in the Potomac River, Virginia, via Barbados before 1718. [PRO.CO5.1443]

JACKIE, master Dugald Thomson, from Port Glasgow to Newfoundland in August 1774. [NAS.E504.28.23]

JACKIE, Captain Bog, bound from the Clyde to Wilmington, was captured by the French and taken to Brest in 1795. [AJ#2459]

JAMAICA PACKET OF BURNTISLAND, 80 tons, Plantation built, master Alexander Glassford, from Leith via Madeira to Jamaica in April 1742, [AJ#224]; master Robert Smith, from Kirkcaldy *with*

22 passengers bound for Antigua in October 1774,
[PRO.T47/12]; master Thomas Smith, from
Kirkcaldy to Brunswick, North Carolina *with 20
passengers* in June 1775. [NAS.E504.20.8]

JAMAICA OF GREENOCK, master Dugald Campbell,
from Greenock to Jamaica in August 1774; master
John Denniston, from Greenock to Antigua in
January 1779; master Edward Kerr, from Port
Glasgow to Jamaica in September 1783.
[NAS.E504.15.24/30] [NAS.E504.22.39]

JAMES OF WAIRWATER, master John Stevenson, from
Port Glasgow to the Caribbean on 15 February
1682. [NAS.E72.19.6]

JAMES OF CRAWFORDYKE, from the Clyde to America
around 1696. [NAS.RD3.144.330]

JAMES OF GREENOCK, master James Scott, from
Greenock via Cork to Barbados on 19 October
1728. [EEC#559]

JAMES OF GLASGOW, master James Gordon, from
Greenock via Cork to Madeira and Virginia, 12
November 1728. [EEC#560]

JAMES OF DUNDEE, a 70 ton brigantine, master John
Traill, arrived in Dundee on 16 October 1742 from
Boston, New England; from Dundee to Virginia in
March 1743; arrived in Dundee on 3 February 1744
from Virginia and Maryland; master Robert
Crawford, from Leith to the Potomac in May 1744;
from Leith to Virginia in March 1748.
[NAS.E504.11.1; E504.28.1/2; CE70.1.2]

JAMES, Captain Wotherspoon, from Greenock to St
Martin's, Dutch West Indies, on 4 November 1752.
[AJ#253]

JAMES, 350 tons, from Stornaway *with passengers* to
Prince Edward Island in 1811. [Inverness
Journal,23.3.1811]

JAMES AND AGNES, from Glasgow *with passengers* to Kingston, Jamaica, on 10 April 1819. [EEC#16824]

JAMES AND DAVID, a brig, master James Cairns, from Dundee on 15 April 1810 bound for Quebec and Montreal. [PC#69]

JAMES AND JANET, master William Muir, from Leith to Philadelphia in July 1747. [NAS.E504.28.2]

JAMES AND MARGARET OF IRVINE, master Hugh Steel, from Greenock to Barbados in February 1747. [NAS.E504.15.3]

JAMES MAURY, master William Candler, from Greenock to New York on 10 August 1825. [DPCA#1200]

JAMIESON OF LEITH, 120 tons, master John Aitken, arrived in Charleston, South Carolina, on 4 January 1763 via Lisbon, [PRO.CO5.510]; from Leith to Philadelphia in August 1763 [NAS.E504.22.10]; arrived in Boston on 22 August 1765 *with passengers* from Leith. [PAB]

JANE, master John McMaster, arrived in Boston on 9 June 1719 *with passengers* from Glasgow and Belfast. [Boston News Letter, 15 June 1719]

JANE OF ANSTRUTHER, a 105 ton brig, master John Smith, arrived in Charleston, South Carolina, on 30 January 1766 from Leith. [PRO.CO5.511]

JANE, master John Thomson, from Port Glasgow to North Carolina in November 1783; master Joseph Watson, from Port Glasgow to North Carolina in August 1784. [NAS.E504.28.36/37]

JANE, Captain Moodie, from the Clyde to Quebec in April 1798. [EWJ#15]

JANET OF LEITH, master Robert Hay, from Leith to the West Indies in 1611. [NAS.E71.29.6/22]

JANET OF GLASGOW, master William Cunningham, from Greenock to Jamaica in January 1776; from Greenock to Jamaica in January 1777; master James Laurie, from Greenock to Jamaica in February 1778. [NAS.E504.15.26/27/29]

JANET OF ABERDEEN, foundered off the Banks of Newfoundland on 19 May 1828. [DPCA#1351]

JANET AND ANN, 140 tons, master George Craik, from Aberdeen *with passengers* to Jamaica on 10 April 1769; from Aberdeen *with passengers* to Grenada in April 1770; master John Youll, from Aberdeen *with passengers* to Grenada and Jamaica in 1773; from Aberdeen *with passengers* to Grenada and Tobago in January 1775.
[AJ#1109/1156/1307/1399]

JANET AND MALLY, master Duncan Ferguson, from Greenock to Antigua in February 1759,
[NAS.E504.15.9]

JEAN OF LARGS, master Ninian Gibson, from Port Glasgow to the West Indies on 26 April 1684.
[NAS.E72.19.9]

JEAN, 100 tons, master John McArthur, from Greenock *with passengers* to Boston, New England, in August 1721. [EEC#413]

JEAN OF PORT GLASGOW, master Colin Dunlop, from Greenock to Virginia 22 February 1728, storm damaged west of 'Izeland' returned to port on 15 March 1728; sailed for Virginia 1 May 1728.
[EEC#338/438/489]

JEAN OF GREENOCK, master John Easdale, from Greenock to Jamaica and return in 1730.
[NAS.AC9.1104]

JEAN, Captain Clark, from Greenock via Madeira to Barbados on 12 March 1748, [CM#4277]; Captain Barbour, from Greenock to Barbados on 8 April 1749. [AJ#68]

JEAN OF PORT GLASGOW, master John Maxwell, from Port Glasgow to Virginia in March 1752. [NAS.E504.28.5]

JEAN OF GLASGOW, at Bermuda, 1753. [NAS.RH#6444]

JEAN, Captain Wilson, from Greenock to St Kitts in December 1758. [AJ#572]

JEAN OF AYR, master John Johnstone, from Ayr to Grenada in February 1769; master John Smith, from Ayr to Antigua in April 1770. [NAS.E504.4.5]

JEAN OF ELIE, master James Burns, from Leith to St Kitts in December 1775. [NAS.E504.22.20]

JEAN OF GREENOCK, master David Taylor, from Greenock to Barbados in August 1776. [NAS,E504.15.26]

JEAN, master James Young, from Greenock to Antigua in December 1779; master William Chisholm, from Greenock to Antigua in September 1782. [NAS.E504.15.32/36]

JEAN, master David Hunter, from Greenock to Newfoundland in March 1781. [NAS.E504.33]

JEAN, a 178 ton brig, master William Paton, from Glasgow *with passengers* to New York in May 1827, arrived in New York on 11 August 1827. [DPCA#1293]

JEAN, 480 tons, master Allan Briggs, from Leith *with passengers* bound for Quebec on 3 April 1828. [S.XII.855]

JEAN AND BETTY, Captain Smith, from Greenock to St
     Kitts on 7 December 1751; from Greenock to St
     Kitts on28 April 1753; from Greenock to Jamaica in
     May 1754; from Greenock to St Kitts on 8 May
     1756; from Greenock to St Kitts in December 1758;
     master Patrick Gordon, from Greenock to St Kitts in
     December 1765.
     [AJ#207/278/330/436/571][NAS.E504.15.13]

JEAN AND MARY OF BOSTON, master James Watson,
     from Greenock *with passengers* to Boston, New
     England, in August 1721; from Greenock *with
     passengers* to Boston on 10 August 1722.
     [EEC#449/566][Burgess Roll of Glasgow]

JEAN AND MAY, master John Rodger, from Port
     Glasgow to Maryland in April 1751, and in May
     1752 [NAS.E504.28.5]

JEANIE, master John Barclay, from Greenock to
     Jamaica in January 1782; from Greenock to
     Jamaica in August 1782; master Thomas Bolton,
     from Greenock to Jamaica in July 1784.
     [NAS.E504.15.35/36/38]

JEANIE, master William McGill, from Port Glasgow to
     Virginia in February 1784 and in April 1785.
     [NAS.E504.22.37/39]; 250 tons, master William
     Kinneir, from Port Glasgow *with passengers*
     bound for Quebec in March 1787. [GMerc:12.1786]

JEANY, master James Orr, from Greenock to St Kitts in
     January 1760; master Archibald Williamson, from
     Greenock via Cape Verde to Barbados in April
     1765; master James Lyon, from Greenock via Cork
     to St Kitts in September 1765.
     [NAS.E504.15.9/12/13]

JEANY, a snow, master Hector Orr, arrived in Boston on
     17 August 1767 *with 22 passengers* from
     Glasgow, also arrived on 1 June 1768 *with
     passengers* from Glasgow; arrived in Boston on 31

October 1766 *with passengers* from Glasgow.
[PAB]

JENNY, Captain Aitken, from Greenock to Jamaica on 8
February 1752. [AJ#216]

JENNY OF GREENOCK, 130 tons, master Donald
Hyndman, arrived in Charleston on 12 March 1759
from Glasgow. [PRO.CO5.510]

JENNY OF GREENOCK, an 80 ton brig, master Robert
Ewing, from Greenock to Antigua in August 1766;
arrived in Charleston, South Carolina, on 22
December 1766 via Antigua; master Alexander
Kerr, from Greenock via Cork to Antigua in
September 1774.
[NAS.E504.15.13/24][PRO.CO5.511]

JENNY, master Hugh Morris, from Irvine bound for
Maryland in May 1765; master Robert Caldwell,
from Irvine bound for Quebec in February 1767;
master James Boyd, from Irvine bound for
Charleston, South Carolina, in October 1767.
[NAS.E504.18.5/6]

JENNY, master Thomas Alexander, from Greenock to
Antigua in July 1776; master William Steel, from
Greenock to Antigua in December 1779; from
Greenock to Antigua in December 1781; master
Niven Linn, from Greenock to Antigua; master
William Steel, from Greenock to Antigua in January
1783; from Greenock to Antigua in January 1784;
from Greenock to Antigua in January 1786.
[NAS,E504.15.26/32/35/36/37/38/42]

JENNY OF GLASGOW, master Robert Kerr, from
Greenock to Jamaica in April 1777; master John
Reid, from Greenock to Dominica in March 1779.
[NAS.E504.15.27/29]

JENNY OF IRVINE, master William Steel, from Greenock
to Antigua in November 1778; from Greenock to
Antigua in November 1784. [NAS.E504.15.30/40]

JENNY, master Robert Muir, from Greenock to Jamaica in March 1784; from Greenock to Jamaica in March 1786. [NAS.E504.15.38/42]

JENNY, master John Tarbert, from Port Glasgow to Jamaica and Grenada in December 1783; master William Bell, from Port Glasgow to North Carolina in October 1784. [NAS.E504.28.36/38]

JERVISWOOD, a snow, master Thomas Baillie, arrived in Charleston, South Carolina, in January 1735. [SCGaz#52]

JOANNA, master John Woodrop, from Port Glasgow to Virginia in November 1751. [NAS.E504.28.5]

JOANNA, master James Brown, from Greenock to Antigua *with passengers* on 9 September 1790. [NAS.E504.15.56]

JOHANNA OF ABERDEEN, 130 tons, from Aberdeen to Virginia in 1711. [Scots Courant, 13.4.1711]

JOHANNA OF NORTH BRITAIN, 100 tons, master Robert Harrison, in Charleston, South Carolina, in February 1727. [PRO.CO5.509]

JOHN OF GLASGOW, master John Denniston, from Greenock to Virginia 13 March 1728. [EEC#448]

JOHN OF PORT GLASGOW, Captain Berry, from Greenock to Barbados on 4 April 1741. [CM#3282]

JOHN OF BO'NESS, a 130 ton snow, master Archibald McMillan, arrived in Charleston, South Carolina, on 11 February 1766 from Bo'ness. [PRO.CO5.511]

JOHN OF KIRKCUDBRIGHT, master John Paul (Jones), in the West Indies 1770. [NAS.SC16.12.14][NAS.RH1.2.697]

JOHN, master Alexander Davies, from Port Glasgow to Port Roseway, Nova Scotia, in May 1784. [NAS.E504.28.37]

JOHN, master John Dunnet, from Port Glasgow to Jamaica in October 1784. [NAS.E504.28.37]

JOHN AND ANN OF IRVINE, master John Service, from Greenock to Barbados in February 1748. [NAS.E504.15.3][CM#4226]; captured by a French privateer and taken to Bayonne on 2 April 1748. [AJ#31]

JOHN AND EDWARD, an American brig, Captain Greenleaf, from Glasgow *with passengers* bound for New York in May 1824. [DPCA#1133]

JOHN AND DAVID OF PORT GLASGOW, a snow, from Glasgow to Barbados by 1728. [NAS.AC10.138]

JOHN AND MARJORY OF MONTROSE, master John Sangster, from Montrose to Jamaica on 19 January 1747. [NAS.E504.24.1]

JOHN AND MATTY OF BELFAST, master John Russell, from Campbeltown to Antigua in January 1776. [NAS.E504.8.5]

JOHN AND ROBERT OF GOUROCK, 60 tons, arrived in Charleston on 4 January 1727 from Glasgow, [PRO.CO6/509]; master Thomas Clark, from Greenock *with 26 convicts from Edinburgh and Glasgow* for South Carolina on 23 October 1728; master Robert Scott, in Charleston during March 1727. [EEC#559] [PRO.CO5.509]; master James Orr, from Greenock to Virginia on 14 March 1741. [CM#3273]

JUDITH, Captain Sedgwick, arrived in Maryland in May 1756 from Glasgow. [MdGaz#577]

JUNO OF GREENOCK, master George Orr, from Greenock to Jamaica in October 1777.

[NAS.E504.15.28]; master Thomas Ritchie, from Greenock *with passengers* via Madeira to Kingston Jamaica, in December 1786. [GM:12.1786]

JUPITER OF ABERDEEN, a snow, master Arthur Gibbon, from Aberdeen *with passengers* to Kingston, Jamaica, on 30 April 1761. [AJ#681/690]

JUPITER OF GLASGOW, master Alexander Buyers, from Greenock to Tobago in March 1778. [NAS.E504.15.29]

KATE, a 118 ton brig, master John Boyack, from Dundee *with passengers* to Charleston, South Carolina, in October 1816. [DPCA#735]

KATHERINE OF NEW YORK, master James Devereux, from Kirkwall, Orkney, to New York 4 August 1753. [NAS.E504.26.2]

KATTIE, master James Clerk, from Greenock to Dominica in July 1777; master John McLennachan, from Greenock to Barbados in October 1781; from Greenock to St Lucia in July 1782. [NAS.E504.15.28/34/36]

KATY, master Robert Gemmill, from Irvine bound for Boston, New England, in August 1766; master Patrick Montgomery, from Irvine bound for Falmouth, New England, in May 1767. [NAS.E504.18.6]

KEITH, a 140 ton snow, master John Baylie, arrived in Charleston, South Carolina, on 30 January 1759 from Glasgow. [PRO.CO5.510]

KENNEDY, Captain Gillies, from Greenock to Barbados on 4 April 1752; master James Montgomery, from Irvine bound for Quebec in May 1767; master James Montgomery, from Irvine bound for St Christopher's and Georgia in September 1771; master James Montgomery, from Irvine bound for

St Christopher's and Georgia in September 1772.
[AJ#224] [NAS.E504.18.6/7]

KENT OF WHITEHAVEN, master Joseph Kelsick, from
Greenock to Virginia on 5 April 1721. [EEC#365]

KILMAURS, Captain Boyd, from Greenock to Jamaica in
January 1755. [AJ#368]

KING GEORGE OF LONDON, master George Grisson,
from Scotland to Jamaica in 1714. [NAS.E508.7.6]

KING GEORGE I, master William Coats, from Gravesend
via Orkney to Richmond Fort, Hudson's Bay, and
return in 1751; master Joseph Spurrell, from
Gravesend via Orkney to Moose, Hudson's Bay,
and return in 1752, also in 1753, 1754, and 1755.
[HBCA#SM32/33]

KING GEORGE II, master Joseph Spurrell, from
Gravesend via Orkney to York Factory, Hudson's
Bay, and return in 1761, 1762, 1763; master
Jonathan Fowler, from Gravesend via Orkney to
York Factory or Churchill, Hudson's Bay, and return
in 1764, 1768, 1769, 1770, 1771, 1772, 1773,
1774, 1775, 1776, 1777, 1778, 1779, 1780.
[HBCA#2M33/34/35/36]

KING GEORGE III, master Joseph Richards, from
Gravesend via Orkney to Moose, Hudson Bay, and
return in 1781; master Jonathan Fowler, from
Gravesend via Orkney to York Factory, Hudson
Bay, and return in 1782; master William
Christopher, from Gravesend via Orkney to Moose
and Churchill, York Factory, Hudson Bay, and
return in 1784, 1785, 1786, 1787, 1788; master
Joshua Turnstall, from Gravesend via Orkney to
York Factory, Hudson Bay, in 1789; Master John
Richards, from Gravesend via Orkney to Moose,
Hudson Bay, and return in 1791, 1792, 1793, 1794,
1795, 1796, 1797, 1798, 1799, and 1800; master
Henry Hanwell, from Gravesend via Orkney to York
Factory, Hudson's Bay, and return in 1801; master

John Turner, from Gravesend via Orkney to York Factory, Hudson Bay, and return in 1802, 1803, 1804, 1805, 1806, 1807, 1808, 1809, 1810, 1812. [HBCA#2M36/37/38/39/40/41/ 42/43]

KING OF PRUSSIA OF GREENOCK, a 40 ton brig, master William Hume, arrived in Charleston, South Carolina, on 4 February 1760 via St Kitts. [PRO.CO5.510]

KINGSTON OF GLASGOW, master Adam Chisholm, from Port Glasgow via Cork to St Kitts in October 1742; from Greenock via Cork to St Kitts on 8 November 1746; from Greenock to St Kitts in December 1747; from Greenock to St Kitts in March 1750; from Greenock to St Kitts on 9 February 1751; from Greenock to St Kitts on 19 December 1753; from Greenock to St Kitts on 28 December 1754; from Glasgow to St Kitts in March 1756; from Greenock to St Kitts on 8 January 1757; master John Campbell, from Greenock to Jamaica in March 1765. [NAS.E504.128.1] [CM#4071] [AJ#119/164/311/365/425/471][NAS.E504.15.3/12]

KINGSTON, master John Tarbert, from Greenock to St Vincent in November 1784; from Greenock to Grenada in November 1785. [NAS.E504.15.40/42]

KINNOULL OF LEITH, a 100 ton snow, master Alexander Alexander, from Leith to St Kitts in October 1765; in Charleston June 1766; arrived in Charleston on 10 January 1767 from Leith; arrived in Charleston on 17 September 1767 via London. [NAS.E504.22.12][PRO.CO5.511]

KIRKCONNELL OF DUMFRIES, from Annan via Whitehaven and Londonderry to Barbados and Virginia in 1710-1711. [PRO.HCA#15/20]; from Dumfries *with passengers* to Virginia in January 1715. [DGA.GF4.19A.10]

KITTY OF IRVINE, a 100 ton snow, master Patrick Montgomerie, arrived in Charleston, South

Carolina, on 5 February 1766 via Antigua.
[PRO.CO5.511]

KOULI KAN, a 90 ton brigantine, master Laurence
McGilchrist, from Port Glasgow via Cork *with
passengers* to Jamaica in October 1746, and on 5
September 1747. [CM#4049/4163/4201]

LADY CHARLOTTE, master Benjamin Moore, from Port
Glasgow to Jamaica in December 1784.
[NAS.E504.28.38]

LADY WALLACE OF AYR, master William Fleck, from
Ayr to Antigua in April 1775. [NAS.E504.4.6]

LAMB OF WORKINGTON, master William Gartskel,
from Greenock to Jamaica in May 1747.
[NAS.E504.15.3]

LARK OF LONDON, master George Rodgers, from
Scotland to Jamaica in 1728. [NAS.E508.22.6]

LARK, master John Kennedy, from Port Glasgow via
Waterford to Newfoundland in April 1773.
[NAS.E504.28.22]

LARK OF IRVINE, master John Fulton, from Greenock to
Grenada in January 1776. [NAS.E504.15.26]

LATONA, Captain Craig, from Dundee *with passengers*
to Quebec on 15 April 1817. [DPCA#768]

LAUREL OF ABERDEEN, master John Coutts, from
Aberdeen *with passengers* via London to
Kingston, Jamaica, in April 1752. [AJ#219]

LAUREL, Captain Laing, from Greenock to St Kitts in
December 1758. [AJ#573]

LAUREL, 171 tons, Captain Spinks, from Dundee to
Kingston, Jamaica, on 18 October 1820. [MC#50];
master George Caithness, from Dundee *with*

passengers bound for New York in February 1823. [DPCA#1072]

LEAH OF GLASGOW, master William Andrews, arrived in Hampton, Virginia, from Glasgow in 18 March 1745 *with passengers*. [MdGaz#5]; arrived in Montrose on 28 August 1745 from the James River, Virginia. [NAS.E504.24.1]

LEAH OF GLASGOW/LONDON, master William Andrew, arrived in Montrose on 28 August 1745 from the James River, Virginia; master David Fraser, arrived in Montrose on 30 June 1748 from the James River, Virginia. [NAS.E504.24.1]

LEATHLY, master John Lickley, arrived in Annapolis, Maryland, in September 1749 from Aberdeen; from Annapolis to Aberdeen in July 1750; arrived in Annapolis in June 1751 from Aberdeen; from Annapolis to Aberdeen in September 1751; arrived in Annapolis in September 1754 from Aberdeen. [MdGaz#230/272/323/335/488]

LEDA, a 200 ton brig, master James Lyall, from Dundee to New York on 17 June 1828. [DPCA#1345]

LEITH GALLEY, master John Sharp, from Leith to Jamaica on 9 February 1755. [AJ#371]

LIBERTY OF BOSTON, 80 tons, master Hugh Smellie, arrived in Charleston, South Carolina, on 30 November 1764 from Greenock (?) [PRO.CO5.511]; master Hugh Smellie, from Greenock to St Kitts in February 1770, [NAS.E504.15.18]

LIBERTY, a brig, Captain Walker, arrived in New York in August 1784 *with 150 passengers* from Glasgow. [MdGaz#1965]

LILLIE OF GLASGOW, a brigantine, from Glasgow to the West Indies in 1726. [NAS.AC9.1098]

LILLY OF GLASGOW, from Port Glasgow to Virginia in January 1746. [NAS.E504.28.2]

LILLY, Captain White from Glasgow bound for the Chesapeake 18 July 1757. [MdGaz#651]

LILLY OF GLASGOW, master James Lyon, from Greenock to St Kitts in January 1770. [NAS.E504.15.18]

LILLY'S PRIZE OF GLASGOW, from Glasgow to South Carolina in 1746, captured by the Spanish and taken to St Augustine. [SM.VIII.449]

LION, master Colin Campbell, from Port Glasgow bound for the Potomac River, Virginia, in February 1787. [GMerc:12.1786]

LISLE OF LEITH, seized in Virginia before 1718. [PRO.HCA#14/68]

LITTLE DONALD OF LEITH, a 70 ton brigantine, arrived in Charleston, South Carolina, on 26 September 1759 from Greenock. [PRO.CO5.510]

LITTLE KATE, Plantation built, master Thomas Boyd, from Greenock to Barbados in February 1786. [NAS.E504.15.42]

LITTLE PAGE OF GLASGOW, master Thomas Hindman, from Greenock to Virginia on 5 April 1721; master Robert Wilson, arrived in Greenock on 5 October 1728 from Virginia. [EEC#365/554]

LITTLE WILLIAM OF LEITH, a 250 ton French prize, master John Murray, from Leith to Virginia in July 1758. [NAS.E504.22.8]

LORD BELHAVEN, Captain McAulay, from Greenock to St Domingo on 2 May 1819. [EEC#16836]

LORD ELDON, a brig, master J. Cooper, from Dundee *with passengers* to New York on 9 June 1827. [DPCA#1293]

LORD FREDERICK, master Robert Eason, from Greenock to Barbados in December 1764; master Robert Wright, from Greenock to Tortula, the Virgin Islands, in April 1779. [NAS.E504.15.12/31]

LORD MONTGOMERIE, arrived in Greenock 22 August 1728 from Virginia. [EEC#532]

LORD MONTGOMERY OF GLASGOW, 80 tons, master John Clark, arrived in Charleston, South Carolina, on 25 January 1732 from Glasgow. [PRO.CO5.509]

LORD WELLINGTON, a 150 ton brig, from Dundee *with passengers* to Quebec and Montreal in March 1816. [DPCA#710]

LOUDOUN OF GLASGOW, 140 tons, Captain Cuddie, from Greenock via Cork to St Kitts on 3 January 1757. [AJ#470]; master Andrew Lyon, arrived in Charleston, South Carolina, on 31 March 1763 from Glasgow. [GaGaz:14.4.1763][PRO.CO5.510]

LOUISA, Captain Oswald, from Glen Elg, Argyll, *with passengers* bound for Quebec in July 1819. [EEC#16865]

LOVELY BETSY, a schooner, master William Hayman, arrived in Boston, New England, on 7 August 1766 *with passengers* from Scotland. [PAB]

LOYALTY OF GLASGOW, master Patrick Cheap, from Glasgow to Guinea and Barbados, pre 1721, captured by pirates on the return voyage. [NAS.AC9.769]

LUCEA, master Robert Hunter, from Greenock to Jamaica in November 1784; from Greenock to Jamaica in October 1786. [NAS.E504.15.40/43]

LUCIA OF WHITEHAVEN, master Samuel Bowman, arrived in Greenock on 22 August 1728 from Virginia. [EEC#532]

LUCRETIA, Captain Fleming, from Greenock to St Kitts in March 1748. [CM#4277]

LUNE, Captain Shirreff, from Leith *with passengers* bound for Jamaica in February 1821, also in October 1821. [EEC#17101/17211]

LYDIA, master Thomas Watson, from Port Glasgow to Virginia in July 1784. [NAS.E504.28.37]

LYDIA, 654 tons, from Dundee to Quebec in May 1808. [DPCA#352]

LYON OF AYR, master David Ferguson, from the West Indies bound for Ayr, wrecked on the coast of Ireland in 1705. [NAS.AC7.12.994-1014]

LYON OF IRVINE, master William Gardner, from Greenock to Barbados in March 1747. [NAS.E504.15.3][CM#4134]

LYON OF LEITH, 120 tons, master Keith Reid, from Leith to Grenada in October 1774. [NAS.E504.22.19]

LYON, master Colin Campbell, from Port Glasgow to Halifax in April 1783; master John Donaldson, from Port Glasgow to Virginia in April 1784; master Colin Campbell, from Port Glasgow to Virginia in February 1785; master John Donaldson, from Port Glasgow to Charleston, South Carolina, in December 1785. [NAS.E504.22.36/37/38/40]

MACFARLANE, master James Peadie, from Port Glasgow *with passengers* bound for Jamaica on 21 April 1740. [CM#3262/3289]

MAGDALENE, master William Carse, from Leith to South Carolina in November 1744. [NAS.E504.22.1]; master James McKenzie, from Leith to Carolina on

23 November 1747, *"The ship Magdalene, Captain James Mackenzie, commander, is to sail from Leith about the first of November next for Charles Town in South Carolina. Any person designed for the said place may have their passage on easy terms. The ship has good accommodation in the cabin and steerage and is well fitted and provided."*. [NAS.AC10.323][CM#4215/4231]

MAGDALENE OF DUNBAR, 110 tons, master Robert Beattie, arrived in Charleston, South Carolina, on 20 November 1764 from Dunbar; arrived in Charleston on 24 November 1766 from Dunbar. [PRO.CO5.511]

MAINWARING, a schooner, master John Davidson, from Gravesend via Orkney to York Factory, Hudson's Bay, and return in 1807. [HBCA#2M47]

MAJESTIC, 311 tons, from Leith *with passengers* bound for Quebec in June 1828, *'maps of the Province of Upper Canada and plans of each separate township will be shewn.'* [S.XII.869]

MALAY, Captain Young, from Greenock to Kingston, Jamaica, on 10 June 1819. [EEC#16853]

MALLY OF CRAWFORDDYKE, master John Pettigrew, arrived in Fort William, Inverness-shire, from Virginia in October 1740. [CM#3217]

MALLY OF GLASGOW, master Alexander Butcher, arrived in Annapolis, Maryland, in August 1750, [MdGaz#278]; from Port Glasgow to Virginia in October 1750; from Annapolis to Glasgow on 28 November 1750, [MdGaz#292]; master James Orr, from Port Glasgow to Virginia in February 1752; master John Crawford, from Port Glasgow to Virginia in August 1752; from Greenock to Barbados in December 1753; from Greenock via Cork to Barbados in October 1754. [NAS.E504.28.1/5][AJ#310/359]

MALLY, Captain Langmuir, from Greenock to St Kitts in December 1758. [AJ#575]

MALLY, master John Mackie, from Irvine to Barbados in May 1783. [NAS.E504.18.10]

MALLY, master John Lawmont, from Port Glasgow to Barbados in July 1784. [NAS.E504.28.37]

MALVINA OF ABERDEEN, master John Smith, from Aberdeen *with 12 passengers* bound for Canada in April 1811. [NAS.E504.1.24]

MANNIE, master Hugh Douglas, from Greenock to Tortula, the Virgin Islands, in January 1782. [NAS.E504.15.35]

MARGARET OF LEITH, master Ebenezer Hathorn, to the West Indies by 1718. [NAS.AC9.626]

MARGARET, Captain Gordon, from Glasgow bound for the Chesapeake 18 July 1758. [MdGaz#651]

MARGARET, master Robert Kerr, from Greenock to Tobago in May 1783; master James How, from Greenock to Tortula in November 1784; master John Livingston, from to Barbados in April 1786. [NAS.E504.15.38/40/43]

MARGARET OF PERTH, a 300 ton brig, master Robert Barclay, from Dundee *with passengers* to Kingston, Jamaica, on 24 December 1815. [DPCA#693/700]

MARGARET, Captain Paterson, from Greenock to Grenada on 22 April 1819. [EEC#16832]

MARGARET BOGLE, 340 tons, master J. C. Portess, from Glasgow *with passengers* bound for New York in May 1824. [DPCA#1133]

MARIA OF NEW YORK, master Thomas Randall, from Kirkwall, Orkney, to New York 30 August 1749. [NAS.E504.26.2]

MARIA, Captain Wallace, from Greenock to Montego Bay, Jamaica, on 20 May 1819. [EEC#16844]

MARJORY OF BO'NESS, master William Boyle, from Leith *with servants* to Jamaica on 23 December 1734. [CM#2281/2297]

MARJORY AND JANET OF KINCARDINE, 50 tons, master John Brown, from Leith to St Kitts in February 1763, [NAS.E504.22.10]

MARLBOROUGH OF GREENOCK, master Thomas Howe, from Greenock to Antigua in March 1779. [NAS.E504.15.30]

MARQUIS OF WELLINGTON, Captain Killing, from Greenock to St Thomas, Danish West Indies, on 21 April 1819. [EEC#16882]

MARS, a privateer, master James Weir, from Port Glasgow *with passengers* to St Kitts and Guadaloupe on 6 October 1760. [AJ#665]

MARS, Captain Mitchell, from Greenock to Jamaica on 25 February 1819; from Glasgow via St Thomas to New Orleans in September 1825. [EEC#16908][DPCA#1208]

MARTHA OF GLASGOW, master William Dunlop, from Greenock bound for Bordeaux and Virginia in December 1727; arrived in Greenock on 14 October 1728 from Virginia. [EEC#405/555]

MARTHA, master John Wilson, from Greenock to Jamaica in August 1782; from Greenock to Jamaica in May 1783; master John Boyle, from Greenock to Jamaica in April 1784; from Port Glasgow to Jamaica in April 1785. [NAS.E504.15.36/38][NAS.E504.28.39]

MARTHA AND SALLY OF MONTROSE, 80 tons, master William Wilkie, arrived in Charleston, South Carolina, on 16 October 1736 via London. [PRO.CO5.510]

MARTIN OF GLASGOW, master Robert Watson, from Greenock to Antigua in May 1747. [NAS.E504.15.3][CM#4158]

MARY OF MONTROSE, master James Stratton, arrived in Montrose on 5 October 1727 from Philadelphia; from Montrose to Maryland on 8 February 1728. [NAS.CE53.1.1]

MARY OF GLASGOW, master Andrew Turner, from Greenock to Virginia on 14 March 1741, also on 7 November 1741. [CM#3273/3374]

MARY OF DUNBARTON, master William Smith, from Greenock via Ireland to Barbados in February 1745. [NAS.E504.15.2]

MARY, Captain MacMillan, from Greenock to Jamaica on 29 December 1750; Captain Hamilton, from Greenock to St Kitts on 19 December 1753; Captain Fleming, from Greenock via Cork to St Kitts on 28 December 1754. [AJ#158/311/365]

MARY OF GLASGOW, master Neil Campbell or Archibald McLarty, from Glasgow to the Small Isles, from there *with passengers* in June 1754 bound for Williamstown, Cape Fear, North Carolina, via Philadelphia, arrived at Cape Fear on 2 October 1754, and returned to Scotland via St Kitts. [NAS.GD64.5.21-22]

MARY OF NEW YORK, master Samuel Broadhurst, from Kirkwall, Orkney Islands, to New York 7 August 1750. [NAS.E504.26.2]

MARY, Captain Crawford, from Greenock to Jamaica on 8 February 1752. [AJ#216]

MARY OF INVERNESS, a 70 ton brigantine, master Alexander Johnston, arrived in Charleston, South Carolina, via Bristol on 5 June 1764. [PRO.CO5.510]

MARY, a snow, master William Welchman, arrived in Boston, New England, on 30 May 1767 *with 31 passengers* from Glasgow. [PAB]

MARY OF DUNDEE, master John Ireland, from Dundee via the Canary Islands and Madeira to Jamaica in April 1768. [NAS.E504.11.6]

MARY OF LEITH, 70 tons, master Andrew Mason, from Leith to Jamaica in December 1774; from Leith to Jamaica in January 1776. [NAS.E504.22.19/20]

MARY OF GLASGOW, master William Walkingshaw, from Greenock *with 21 passengers* bound for Jamaica in November 1773; from Greenock to Jamaica in October 1774; from Greenock to Jamaica in November 1776; from Greenock to Jamaica in September 1777; from Greenock to Jamaica in October 1778; from Greenock to Jamaica in October 1779; from Greenock to Jamaica in January 1781; master Francis Roseburgh, from Greenock to Jamaica in January 1782; master Thomas Silk, from Greenock to Antigua in October 1782; from Greenock to Jamaica in January 1783; master Robert Hunter, from Greenock to Jamaica in January 1784; Captain Roxborough, arrived in New York in September 1784 *with passengers* from Greenock. [NAS.E504.15.24/26/28/30/32/33/35/37/38] [MdGaz#1968]

MARY, master Archibald Henry, from Port Glasgow to New York in April 1783. [NAS.E504.22.36]

MARY, [formerly the Governor Dalling], 400 tons, master James Noble, from Port Glasgow *with passengers*

bound for Kingston, Jamaica, in November 1783.
[AJ#1865]

MARY, master John Hartwell, from Port Glasgow to
Philadelphia in December 1783; master Matthew
Brown, from Port Glasgow to St Kitts in December
1784 also in October 1785.
[NAS.E504.28.36/38/40]

MARY OF GREENOCK, master John Fish, from
Greenock to Jamaica in November 1784.
[NAS.E504.15.40]

MARY, a new brigantine, master Thomas Edgar, from
Greenock to Kingston, Morant Bay, etc, Jamaica,
in January 1787, *"Wanted for Jamaica, a house
carpenter and a gardener"*. [GMerc:12.1786]

MARY, Captain Blain, from the Clyde to Jamaica by
1795. [NAS.AC7.67]

MARY OF ABERDEEN, master James Morrison, from
Aberdeen *with 30 passengers* bound for Halifax,
Nova Scotia, in April 1811; from Aberdeen *with 20
passengers* bound for Halifax in April 1812.
[NAS.E504.1.24]

MARY, a schooner, master Robert Small, from Dundee
with passengers to Quebec and Montreal on 23
April 1827. [DPCA#1287]

MARY AND BETTY, 140 tons, master James Melven,
from Aberdeen *with passengers* to Antigua in 21
March 1749. [AJ#54/64]

MARY AND FRANCIS OF WHITEHAVEN, master
Robert Hodgson, arrived in Greenock on 18 August
1728 from Virginia. [EEC#532]

MARY AND JANE, Captain Hall, from Greenock to St
Thomas, Danish West Indies, on 30 January 1819.
[EEC#16797]

MARY AND KATIE OF LEITH, 40 tons, master John Watson, from Leith to Charleston in December 1783. [NAS.E504.22.28]

MARY BEDWARD, master James Noble, from Port Glasgow to Jamaica in October 1783, in November 1784, and in December 1785. [NAS.E504.22.36/38/40]

MASON OF AYR, master William Hunter, from Ayr to Dominica in February 1776. [NAS.E504.4.6]

MATTY, a sloop, master James Gregory, from Port Glasgow to Barbados in February 1742. [NAS.E504.28.1]

MATTY OF GLASGOW, 150 tons, master John Douglas, from Leith to St Kitts in January 1757; master Robert Peacock, from Leith to Maryland in September 1769. [NAS.E504.22.7/15]

MATTY, master Abram Hunter, from Greenock to Bermuda in March 1783; master John Service, from Greenock to Bermuda in October 1784; from Port Glasgow to Bermuda in October 1785. [NAS.E504.15.37/38/40]

MAY OF GLASGOW, master William Watson, arrived in Greenock from Antigua on 8 October 1728. [EEC#554]

MAYFLOWER OF LIVERPOOL, master John Martin, from Port Glasgow to the West Indies on 25 January 1682. [NAS.E72.19.6]

MAYFLOWER OF GLASGOW, master Robert Johnstone, from Port Glasgow to the West Indies on 5 October 1682; master Walter Noble, from Port Glasgow to the Caribbean on 3 March 1685. [NAS.E72.19.9/11]

MAYFLOWER OF WHITEHAVEN, master Edward Tubman, arrived in Greenock on 19 August 1728 from Virginia. [EEC#532]

MAYFLOWER, Captain Steill, from Irvine bound for Barbados, captured by a French privateer and taken to Bayonne on 2 April 1748. [AJ#31]

MAZAREEN OF WHITEHAVEN, master Richard Kelsick, from Greenock to Virginia 29 December 1727; arrived in Greenock on 22 August 1728 from Virginia. [EEC#405/532]

MENIE OF GLASGOW, a 120 ton snow, master Alexander Bain, in Charleston in January 1762. [PRO.CO5.510]

MENNY OF GREENOCK, master Stewart Dow, from Greenock to Jamaica in July 1776; from Greenock to Jamaica in July 1777. [NAS.E504.15.26/28]

MENTOR, master J. L. Wilson, from Greenock *with passengers* to New York on 10 December 1824, [DPCA#1154]

MERCURY OF LONDON, 150 tons, master Robert Stirling, arrived in Charleston, South Carolina, on 16 November 1759 from Dundee. [PRO.CO5.510]

MERCURY OF BO'NESS, master William Robertson, in Charleston, South Carolina, in November 1762. [PRO.CO5.510]

MERCURY OF GLASGOW, master Hugh Hendry, from Greenock to Jamaica in September 1776; master Hannibal Lusk, from Greenock to Tortula, the Virgin Islands, in June 1782; from Greenock to Jamaica in December 1784; from Greenock to Jamaica in February 1786. [NAS.E504.15.26/36/40/42]

MERMAID OF GLASGOW, master John Bowie, from Greenock to Jamaica in February 1776; from Greenock to Jamaica in December 1776; from

Greenock to Jamaica in October 1778.
[NAS.E504.15.26/27/30]

MERMAID OF GREENOCK, master James Cochrane, from Greenock to Barbados in August 1777. [NAS.E504.15.28]

MERMAID, master Robert Hunter, from Port Glasgow to Virginia in July 1784 and in June 1785. [NAS.E504.22.37/39]

MIDAS, a 260 ton brig, master Robert Mawer, from Dundee *with passengers* to Quebec and Montreal on 29 June 1824; from Dundee *with* passengers to Quebec in September 1825; from Dundee *with passengers* to Quebec and Montreal in March 1826; [DPCA#1138/1203/1230]

MINERVA OF DUNDEE, 100 tons, master James Rea, arrived in Charleston, South Carolina, on 22 August 1765 from Dundee; in Charleston during August 1767. [PRO.CO5.511]

MINERVA OF GREENOCK, Plantation built, master James Rankin, from Ayr to Virginia in October 1768; master John McDonald, from Greenock to Tobago in October 1777; master Robert Spears, from Greenock to Jamaica in November 1779; from Greenock to Jamaica in January 1781; from Greenock to Jamaica in March 1782; from Greenock to Jamaica in January 1783; from Greenock to Jamaica in November 1783; from Greenock to Jamaica in December 1784; from Greenock to Jamaica in June 1785; from Greenock to Jamaica in January 1786. [NAS.E504.4.5] [NAS.E504.15.28/32/33/35/37/38/40/41/42]; master Archibald McLarty, from Greenock to Jamaica in January 1787, *"Wanted for Jamaica, a house-carpenter and a gardener, well recommended"*. [GMerc:12.1786]

MINERVA, 300 tons, master William Gibbon, from Aberdeen *with passengers* to Grenada and Tobago in January 1775. [AJ#1400]

MINERVA, master John Boyd, from Port Glasgow to Philadelphia in January 1784. [NAS.E504.28.37]

MINERVA, 211 tons, Captain Barridge, from Greenock *with passengers* to Charleston, South Carolina, in November 1805. [Clyde Commercial Advertiser #10]

MINERVA, master Josiah L. Wilson, from Greenock *with passengers* to New York on 10 September 1824. [DPCA#1144]

MIRIAM, Captain Chisholm, from Greenock to Jamaica on 31 March 1750, [AJ#119]

MISSOURI, a 200 ton American brig, master Peter Bell, from Greenock *with passengers* to Philadelphia in May 1795, *'steerage passage seven guineas'*. [AJ#2468]

MOLLY OF GLASGOW, master John Douglas, from Leith to St Kitts and return in 1757. [NAS.AC7.50]

MOLLY OF DUNBAR, a 40 ton brigantine, master John Middlemass, in Charleston, South Carolina, during August 1758. [PRO.CO5.510]

MOLLY OF GREENOCK, master William Thomson, from Greenock to Jamaica in May 1778. [NAS.E504.15.29]

MONIMIA, master Edward Morrison, from Greenock to St Vincent in February 1777; master Benjamin Muir, from Greenock to Jamaica in November 1777. [NAS.E504.15.27/28]

MONRO OF GLASGOW, 100 tons, master James Glasford, arrived in Charleston, South Carolina, on 4 July 1758 from Glasgow. [PRO.CO.510]

MONTGOMERIE, master David Dunlop, from Port Glasgow to Virginia in November 1748. [NAS.E504.28.4]

MONTGOMERIE OF GLASGOW, a 70 ton snow, master John Wilson, arrived in Charleston, South Carolina, on 23 November 1758 from Glasgow; master Alexander Montgomerie, arrived in Annapolis, Maryland, in December 1759 from Glasgow; master John Wilson, arrived in Charleston on 29 March 1760 from Irvine; arrived in the Patuxent in March 1761 from Glasgow. [MdGaz#762/829]; in Charleston April 1761. [PRO.CO5.510]

MONTROSE OF GLASGOW, a snow, master James Gregory, from Port Glasgow to Antigua in March 1743; master Daniel Graham, arrived in Antigua on 30 April 1748; Captain Graham, from Greenock to Antigua in September 1749; from Greenock to St Kitts on 13 October 1752; from Greenock to St Kitts in August 1753; from Greenock to Jamaica in May 1754; Captain Walkingshaw, from Glasgow to Jamaica in March 1756. [NAS.E504.28.1][AJ#23/92/250/294/330/425]

MONTROSE OF ABERDEEN, Captain Greig, from Aberdeen *with passengers* bound for Antigua in March 1759. [AJ#576/586]

MORNINGFIELD, Captain Laing, from Glen Elg, Argyll, *with passengers* bound for Quebec in July 1819. [EEC#16865]

NANCY, master James Park, from Aberdeen via Norway and Ireland to Maryland on 22 April 1748. [AJ#17]

NANCY OF KIRKCALDY, a 80 ton snow, master Alexander Ritchie, arrived in Charleston, South Carolina, on 27 December 1752 via Bourdeaux. [PRO.CO5.510]

NANCY, master Andrew Anderson, from Greenock to Antigua in October 1765. [NAS.E504.15.13]

NANCY OF IRVINE, a 70 ton snow, master Hugh Brown, in Charleston, South Carolina, in August 1758; arrived in Charleston on 7 May 1759 from Glasgow; arrived in Charleston on 8 May 1760 from Glasgow. [PRO.CO5.510]

NANCY, master Adam McLeish, from Greenock to Grenada in January 1766. [NAS.E504.15.13]; from Port Glasgow to Jamaica in October 1772; master Adam McLeish, from Port Glasgow to Grenada in October 1774; from Port Glasgow to Grenada in October 1775. [NAS.E504.28.21/23]

NANCY OF LEITH, master Robert Miller, from Leith to Grenada in April 1775. [NAS.E504.22.19]

NANCY OF GREENOCK, master James Clark, from Glasgow to St Kitts and the Bay of Honduras in January 1776. [NAS.E504.15.26]

NANCY OF PORT GLASGOW, master Walter Buchanan, from Greenock to Grenada in January 1777; from Greenock *with passengers* bound for St Vincent in January 1778. [NAS.E504.15.27/29]

NANCY OF GLASGOW, master John Steel, from Port Glasgow to Jamaica in January 1776, [NAS.E504.28.23]; from Greenock to Jamaica in February 1777; from Greenock to Jamaica in October 1778. [NAS.E504.15.27/30]

NANCY, master Hugh Douglas, from Port Glasgow to Charleston, South Carolina, in December 1783; from Glasgow to Virginia in April 1784. [NAS.E504.28.36][MdGaz#1945]

NANCY OF AYR, master William Fleck, from Ayr to Virginia in December 1784. [NAS.E504.4.8]

NANCY OF GREENOCK, British built, master Archibald McLarty, from Greenock to Jamaica in January 1778; master Andrew Smith, from Greenock to Jamaica and Antigua in August 1786. [NAS.E504.15.29/43]

NANCY, master Robert Muir, from Greenock to Antigua in July 1782. [NAS.E504.15.36]

NANCY, master Abram Hunter, from Greenock to Bermuda in September 1782. [NAS.E504.15.36]

NANNIE OF GLASGOW, 70 tons, master John Lyon, in Charleston, South Carolina, on 1 April 1727. [PRO.CO5/509]

NANTON, master John Vint, from Leith to Antigua in February 1759. [NAS.E504.22.8]

NELLIE OF LEITH, 100 ton, British built, James Crawford, from Leith to Cape Fear, North Carolina, in September 1773. [NAS.E504.22.17]

NELLY OF GLASGOW, master Archibald Hamilton, from Greenock to St Kitts on 25 July 1741. [CM#3332]

NELLY, Captain Baillie, from Greenock via Cork to Jamaica on 1 November 1746. [CM#4068]

NELLY, Captain McKirdy, arrived in Annapolis, Maryland, *with 3 indentured servants [charcoal makers]* from Glasgow in May 1764; arrived in Maryland during October 1767 from Glasgow. [MdGaz#995/1158]

NELLY OF GREENOCK, a 90 ton snow, master John Wilson, arrived in Charleston, South Carolina, on 10 January 1764 via St Martins, Dutch West Indies, and on 29 August 1764 via St Kitts; in Charleston during September 1767. [PRO.CO5.511]

NELLY, master William Brickenridge, from Ayr *with passengers* possibly to Newhaven, Connecticut, in November 1766. [see PRO.AO12.92.5]

NELLY OF GLASGOW, arrived in Virginia on 3 April 1771 via Barbados. [VSS]

NEPTUNE, from Glasgow to Boston, New England, in 1728. [NAS.CS96/3814]

NEPTUNE OF DUMFRIES, 90 tons, master Archibald Graham, in Charleston, South Carolina, during December 1735. [PRO.CO5.509]

NEPTUNE, master James Weir, from Port Glasgow to Virginia in May 1752. [NAS.E504.28.5]

NEPTUNE OF LONDONDERRY, master Norman Harrison Chevers, from Loch Tarbert, Argyll, *with 302 passengers* bound for America in 1770; from Loch Tarbert, Argyll, *with 300 passengers* bound for America in 1771. [NAS.RH1.2.933/ii]

NEPTUNE, master Robert McLeish, from Irvine bound for North Carolina in October 1766. [NAS.E504.18.6]

NEPTUNE OF PORT GLASGOW, 140 tons, master Patrick McKinlay, arrived in Charleston, South Carolina, on 1 February 1766 from Glasgow; arrived in Charleston on 19 November 1766 via Rotterdam. [PRO.CO5.511]

NEPTUNE, Captain Bell, from Port Glasgow to Virginia in February 1786. [NAS.E504.28.40]

NESTOR, master John Harrison, from Greenock to Grenada in November 1776. [NAS.E504.15.27]

NEWALL, master Walter Smith, arrived in Annapolis, Maryland, in September 1750 from Glasgow via Hamburg. [MdGaz#282]

NIGHTINGALE OF WHITEHAVEN, from Greenock to
Virginia on 25 November 1715. [GCo#2]

NIMBLE, a brig, master Thomas Williamson, from
Gravesend via Orkney to Eastmain and Moose,
Hudson's Bay, in 1792 and 1793. [HBCA#2M50]

NORFOLK, master William Andrew, from Greenock to
Jamaica in March 1765. [NAS.E504.15.12]

NORVAL, a brig, master Alexander Allan, from Dundee
with passengers to Norfolk, Virginia, in May 1815.
[DPCA#666]

NYMPH, Captain Hutchison, from Dundee *with
passengers* to Charleston on 11 April 1817.
[DPCA#768]

OCEAN OF GREENOCK, master William Ambrose, from
Greenock to St Lucia in December 1781; master
Benjamin More, from Greenock to Jamaica in
December 1783. [NAS.E504.15.35/38]

OCEAN, master William Kinneir, from Port Glasgow to
Quebec in February 1786. [NAS.E504.28.40]

OCEAN, a 245 ton brig, Captain Bruce, from Dundee
with passengers to Miramachi or Quebec and
Montreal on 2 April 1824. [DPCA#1121/1132]

OLIVE OF GLASGOW, 100 tons, master James Watson,
from Greenock *with passengers* to Barbados and
the Leeward Islands in September 1721,
[EEC#424]; master Henry Colquhoun, arrived in
Boston in 1726, [NEHGS: MS#B/S36v6]; from
Greenock bound for South Carolina in March 1728.
[EEC#431]

OLIVER OF BELFAST, master Edward McCormick, from
Greenock via Belfast to Antigua in June 1770.
[NAS.E504.15.18]

ORANGE, a 140 ton brig, Captain Paterson, from Dundee *with passengers* to Charleston and New Orleans in January 1817. [DPCA#754]

ORANGEFIELD OF AYR, 100 tons, master Hugh Morris, from Irvine bound for New York in September 1761; arrived in Charleston from Ayr on 4 November 1766. [NAS.E504.18.5][PRO.CO5.511]

PAGE OF IRVINE, master John Fairie, from Port Glasgow to Boston, New England, in February 1748. [NAS.E504.28.3]

PAISLEY, Captain Hyndman, arrived in the Potomac River, Maryland in December 1772 from the Clyde. [MdGaz#1425]

PALLAS OF GLASGOW, master Peter Hamilton, from Greenock to Jamaica in October 1777. [NAS.E504.15.28]

PALLAS, 200 tons, 'a new vessel', from Greenock *with passengers* bound for Antigua in December 1786. [GMerc:12.1786]

PATIENCE AND MARGARET, master John Gowan, from Leith to Philadelphia in August 1748. [NAS.E504.28.2]

PATRICK, master James Patrick, from Dundee *with passengers* to Grenada 26 February 1773. [AJ#1308]

PATRIOT, a 200 ton brig, master Alexander Anderson, from Aberdeen *with 2 passengers* bound for Quebec in February 1812, arrived there in May 1812, [AJ.26.2.1812; QG.30.5.1812]; from Aberdeen *with passengers* to Kingston, Jamaica, in December 1816. [DPCA#747]

PEARL OF HAPTON, 150 tons, master John Francis, arrived in Charleston, South Carolina, on 7 February 1764 from Glasgow, [PRO.CO5.511];

arrived in Maryland from Scotland in June 1765. [MdGaz#1050]

PEGGIE OF GLASGOW, master James Corbett, arrived in Montrose on 2 November 1747 from the Rappahannock River, Virginia; from Montrose on 23 December 1747 to Virginia. [NAS.E504.24.1]

PEGGIE OF DUNDEE, 100 tons, master John Ireland, from Dundee to Cape Fear, North Carolina, 27 February 1766, and in March 1767. [NAS.E504.11.6]

PEGGIE, master Robert Esson, from Greenock to St Lucia in March 1782; master Duncan McRobb, from Greenock to Barbados in April 1784. [NAS.E504.15.35/38]

PEGGIE OF AYR, master Alexander McCoskrie, from Ayr to the James River, Virginia, in February 1784. [NAS.E504.4.8]

PEGGY, Captain Yuill, from Greenock via Cork to St Kitts on 28 December 1754. [AJ#365]

PEGGY OF LEITH, 100 ton, British built, William Paton jr., from Leith to Edenton, North Carolina, on 2 November 1774. [NAS.E504.22.18]

PEGGY OF GLASGOW, a 110 ton snow, master William Craig, arrived in Charleston, South Carolina, on 14 January 1767 from Glasgow; master David McKay, from Greenock to Jamaica in January 1775 and in January 1776.
[PRO.CO5.511][NAS.E504.15.24/26]

PEGGY OF GREENOCK, master Robert Bog, from Greenock to Dominica in May 1776. [NAS.E504.15.26]

PEGGY OF GREENOCK, master Alexander McCaull, from Greenock to Jamaica in June 1776; master George Rees, from Greenock to Newfoundland in

April 1781. [NAS.E504.15.26/33]; master Archibald Whyte, from Greenock via Guernsey to Antigua in December 1782. [NAS.AC9.3184]

PEGGY, master John Duncan, from Port Glasgow to Antigua in October 1783. [NAS.E504.28.36]

PEGGY AND NELLY OF GREENOCK, a 70 ton snow, Captain Boyd, from Greenock to the West Indies on 21 March 1752. [AJ#221]; a 70 ton snow, master Robert Haggart, arrived in Charleston on 30 January 1758 from Glasgow. [PRO.CO5.510]

PELICAN OF SALTCOATS, master Robert Auld, from Saltcoats via Cork to Barbados and Antigua, and return by 1734. [NAS.AC7.40.166]

PENNY, master Robert Salmon, from Port Glasgow to Virginia in June 1785. [NAS.E504.22.39]

PHELIS, master James Ramsay, from Port Glasgow to Maryland in May 1785. [NAS.E504.22.39]

PINKY, a sloop, master Robert Lees, from Port Glasgow *with passengers "joiners, masons and blacksmiths may apply"* bound for Jamaica on 25 April 1741. [CM#3277/3290]

PLANTER OF ABERDEEN, 150 tons, master Robert Ragg, from Aberdeen to Maryland in May 1743; from Aberdeen in May 1744 to Maryland, [NAS.E504.1.1]; master James Elphinstone, from Aberdeen *with passengers* to Antigua on 15 February 1751; Captain Ogilvie, from Aberdeen *with passengers* to Antigua and Jamaica in July 1754; from Cromarty on 1 October 1754, *with 80 passengers*, landed in Antigua on 1 December 1755. [AJ#162/333/348/369]

PLOUGHMAN OF ABERDEEN, a 165 ton brigantine, master Alexander Yule, from Aberdeen *with 28 passengers* bound for Pictou, Nova Scotia, in June 1811; master James Main, from Aberdeen *with 12*

passengers bound for Pictou in March 1812.
[NAS.E504.1.24]

POLLY, Captain Peacock, arrived at Oxford, Maryland,
from Glasgow in September 1763; arrived in
Oxford, Maryland, in July 1765 from Glasgow.
[MdGaz#959/1055]

POLLY, master Robert Craig, from Greenock to St Kitts
in October 1765; master Roger Stewart, from
Greenock to Antigua in March 1777.
[NAS.E504.15.13/27]

POMONA, master Hugh Morris, from Port Glasgow to
Jamaica in February 1784; master James Coutts
Crawford, from Port Glasgow to Charleston, South
Carolina, in November 1785. [NAS.E504.28.37/40]

PORT GLASGOW OF BOSTON, 120 ton snow, master
Archibald Yuill, arrived in Charleston, South
Carolina, on 13 March 1765 from Glasgow.
[PRO.CO5.511]

PORT GLASGOW, Captain McLintock, from Greenock to
Antigua on 1 December 1753; Captain Reid, from
Greenock to Antigua in March 1756. [AJ#309/428]

POTTUXANT, master Hannibal Lusk, from Leith to
Maryland in March 1768. [NAS.E504.22.13]

PRETTY BETSY, Captain Gray, from Greenock to St
Kitts on 12 April 1746. [CM#3982][SM.IX.454]

PRINCE FERDINAND OF GLASGOW, a 70 ton snow,
master John Ryburn, arrived in Charleston, South
Carolina, during February 1760 from Glasgow.
[PRO.CO5.510]

PRINCE GEORGE OF GLASGOW, master Robert
Hamilton, from Greenock to Jamaica on 12
December 1741. [CM#3318]

PRINCE OF WALES, master George Smith, from
Greenock to Barbados in December 1765.
[NAS.E504.15.13]

PRINCE OF WALES I, master Henry Hanwell, from
Gravesend via Orkney to York Factory, Hudson's
Bay, and return in 1793, 1794, 1795, 1796,
1797,1798, 1799, 1800, 1801, 1802, 1803, 1804,
1805, 1806, 1807, 1808, 1809, 1810, 1812, 1813,
1814, 1815, 1817, and 1828; master John Davison,
from Gravesend via Orkney to York Factory,
Hudson's Bay, and return in 1818, 1819, 1820,
1821, 1822, 1823, 1824, 1825, 1826, and 1827.
[HBCA#2M66]

PRINCE RUPERT I, master George Spurrell, from
Gravesend, via Orkney to York Factory, Hudson's
Bay, and return in 1751, 1752, 1753, 1754, 1755;
master Jonathan Fowler, from Gravesend via
Orkney to York Factory, Hudson's Bay, and return
in 1757, 1758, 1759, and 1760. [HBCA#2M90]

PRINCE RUPERT II, master Jonathan Fowler, from
Gravesend via Orkney to Churchill, Hudson's Bay,
and return in 1756, 1757, 1758, 1759, 1760; master
William Norton, from Gravesend via Orkney to
Albany and Moose, Hudson's Bay, and return in
1761, 1762 and 1763; master John Horner, from
Gravesend via Orkney to Albany and Moose,
Hudson's Bay, in 1764; master Joseph Richards,
from Gravesend via Orkney to Churchill, Hudson's
Bay, in 1768. [HBCA#2M90/91/92]

PRINCE RUPERT III, master Joseph Richards, from
Gravesend via Orkney to Churchill, York Factory, or
Moose, Hudson's Bay, and return in 1769, 1770,
1771, 1772, 1773, 1774, 1775, 1777, 1778, 1780;
master Jonathan Fowler, from Gravesend via
Orkney to Churchill, York Factory, Hudson's Bay,
and return in 1781; master William Christopher,
from Gravesend via Orkney to Knapp's Bay,
Churchill, Hudson's Bay, and return in 1782; master
Joshua Turnstall, from Gravesend via Orkney to

Churchill or Moose, Hudson's Bay, and return in 1783, 1784, 1785, and 1786. [HBCA#2M92/93/94/95]

PRINCE RUPERT IV, master Benjamin Bell, from Gravesend via Orkney to Moose, Hudson's Bay, and return in 1827, 1828 and 1829. [HBCA#2M95/96

PRINCESS ROYAL OF GREENOCK, master Cuthbert Kelburn, from Greenock to Grenada and Tobago in November 1774 and in February 1776. [NAS.E504.15.24/26]

PROSPEROUS OF BOSTON, from the Clyde to America around 1696. [NAS.RD3.144.330]

PROSPEROUS OF MONTROSE, master Joseph McIntosh, arrived in Montrose from Maryland in January 1726. [NAS.CE53.1.1]

PROVIDENCE OF GLASGOW, 60 tons, master Henry Fisher, arrived in York, Virginia, on 24 April 1727, via Barbados, [VSS]; master Archibald Dunlop, from Greenock to Philadelphia 18 August 1728. [EEC#532]

PRINCESS MARY OF FALMOUTH, 60 tons, Plantation built, master Arthur Howell, from Leith to Falmouth, New England, 18 September 1772. [E504.22.17]

PROVIDENCE OF LONDON, arrived in Somerset County, Maryland, in 1692 from Scotland. [SPAWI.1692.2295]

PROVIDENCE, master John Martin, arrived in Leith from New York in December 1792, from Leith *with passengers* bound for New York in January 1793. [EdGaz#4]

PSYCHE, a 145 ton brig, master Thomas Erskine, from Dundee *with passengers* to Montreal and Quebec in March 1815; from Dundee **with passengers** to New York in March 1816. [DPCA#657/702]

QUEBEC OF GREENOCK, master Robert Kerr, from Greenock to Grenada in 1780. [NAS.AC7.58]

QUEEN CAROLINA OF WHITEHAVEN, master John Fell, arrived in Greenock on 18 August 1728 from Virginia. [EEC#532]

QUEEN CHARLOTTE, master John Turner, from Gravesend via Orkney to Eastmain, Moose, Churchill and York Factory, Hudson's Bay, in 1790, 1791, 1793, 1794, 1796, 1797, 1798, 1799, and 1800. [HBCA#SM117/118/119/120]

RACHEL OF LEITH, Plantation built, 90 ton, master Thomas Pilland, from Leith to Wilmington 12 May 1775. [NAS.E504.22.19]

RACHEL AND JOHN OF LONDON, from Kelburn, Ayrshire, on 4 March 1686 bound for Antigua, arrived there on 15 May 1686, from Antigua to Port Royal, South Carolina, on 27 July 1686. [Misc. Bound Collections, W C Clements Library, University of Michigan]

RAE GALLEY OF GLASGOW, 120 tons, master Patrick McKinley, arrived in the Upper James River, Virginia, on 7 September 1769 via Antigua. [VSS]

RANGER, master Robert Wright, from Greenock to Barbados in November 1779. [NAS.E504.15.32]

REBECCA, master John McColl, from Greenock to Antigua in October 1782; from Port Glasgow to Halifax, Nova Scotia, in February 1784. [NAS.E504.15.37][NAS.E504.28.37]

REBECCA AND MARY OF MONTROSE, master George Ouchterlonie, arrived in Charleston, South Carolina, on 19 August 1736. [PRO.CO5.510]

RECOVERY OF MARYLAND, from the Clyde to America around 1696. [NAS.RD3.144.330]

RECOVERY, a 204 ton brig, Captain Weatherhead, from Greenock *with passengers* to Baltimore in January 1826. [DPCA#1216]

RENOWN, a barque, master George Watson, from Aberdeen *with passengers* to Jamaica in January 1827. [AJ#4121]

RESTORATION OF LONDON, master James Hall, from Leith *with Palatines* bound for Philadelphia in July 1747. [NAS.E504.28.1][CM#4175]

RETRENCH, a 314 ton brig, master John Cooper, from Greenock *with passengers* to Charleston, South Carolina, in August 1827. [DPCA#1305]

RETURN, a schooner, master Joseph Newall, arrived in Boston, New England, in October 1718 from Glasgow. [Boston News Letter, 24 November 1718]

RICHMOND OF BO'NESS, a 170 ton snow, master James Hamilton, arrived in Charleston, South Carolina, on 1 July 1766 via London. [PRO.CO5.511]

RITCHIE OF GREENOCK, master Robert Hunter, from Greenock to St George's Quay, Bay of Honduras, in November 1774. [NAS.E504.15.24]

ROBERT, a brigantine, master James Ferguson, arrived in Boston, New England, on 4 August 1718 from Glasgow and Belfast. [Boston News Letter, 11 August 1718]

ROBERT OF WHITEHAVEN, master George Griffin, arrived in Greenock on 19 October 1728 from Barbados. [EEC#559]

ROBERT, Captain Shannan, from Greenock via Cork to St Kitts on 29 December 1750. [AJ#158]

ROBERT OF IRVINE, a 80 ton brigantine, master James Boyd, arrived in Charleston, South Carolina, on 20 November 1758 from Glasgow; master James McLean, arrived in Charleston on 7 January 1760 from Irvine. [PRO.CO5.510]

ROBERT OF GREENOCK, 110 tons, master James Rankin, arrived in Charleston, South Carolina, on 5 February 1766 from Greenock. [PRO.CO5.511]

ROBERT OF GLASGOW, 110 tons, master James Rankin, in Charleston, South Carolina, during January 1767; master Alexander Murdoch, from Greenock to Jamaica in February 1778; master John Hartwell, from Greenock to Jamaica in January 1779.
[PRO.CO5.511][NAS.E504.15.29/30]

ROBERT AND ELIZABETH OF IRVINE, an 80 ton brig, master James Boyd, in Charleston, South Carolina, during February 1760. [PRO.CO5.510]

ROBERT AND JOHN, Captain Paterson, from Greenock to Virginia on 19 April 1746. [CM#3983]

ROBERT AND MARY OF KINCARDINE, 100 tons, British built, master Robert Hutchinson, from Leith to Charleston, South Carolina, in February 1785; from Leith to Jamaica and Charleston, South Carolina, on 21 October 1785. [NAS.E504.22.30]

ROGER STEWART, master Robert Kerr, from Greenock *with passengers* to Savannah, Georgia, in August 1827. [DPCA#1305]

ROSAMOND, master Robert Angus, from Port Glasgow to Grenada in March 1785, and in April 1786; *"the very best accommodation for passengers".* [GMerc:12.1786] [NAS.E504.28.38/40]

ROSE, a brigantine, master Archibald Yuill, arrived in Greenock 16 October 1728 from Jamaica. [EEC#559]

ROSE OF GLASGOW, master James Fleming, from Port Glasgow to St Kitts in January 1743. [NAS.E504.28.1

ROSELLE, master Robert Liddle, from Leith *'a few joiners, house-carpenters, millwrights, masons, bricklayers, and blacksmiths who can be well recommended will find good encouragement to go to Jamaica'* to Kingston, Jamaica, in December 1793. [EdAd#3127]; master David Gourlay, from Leith to Jamaica by 1799. [NAS.AC7/72]

ROSEHILL, Captain McColl, from Greenock to Tortula, the Virgin Islands, on 15 May 1821. [EEC#17156]

ROSINA, a brigantine, master Aaron Lithgow, from Dundee *with passengers* to Charleston and New Orleans in December 1825. [DPCA#1214]

ROSINA, a 214 ton brig, from Port Glasgow to Quebec in July 1828. [DPCA#1350]

ROSS, master John Cathcart, from Greenock *with 8 passengers* bound for Jamaica in November 1773. [NAS.E504.15]

ROWLEY, a brig, master Donald McLarty, from Leith *with passengers* bound for Grenada on 19 May 1828. [S.XII.870]

ROYAL WIDOW, master Alexander Ritchie, from Greenock to Jamaica in April 1755; Captain Hutcheson, from Greenock to Jamaica in September 1755. [NAS.E504.15.7][AJ#403]

RUBY OF ABERDEEN, 80 tons, master Alexander Gordon, from Aberdeen to Maryland in March 1743; from Aberdeen to Maryland on 23 April 1746. [NAS.E504.1.1]

RUBY, master James Ramsay, from Greenock to Jamaica in December 1783; from Greenock to Jamaica in February 1785; from Greenock to Jamaica in December 1785. [NAS.E504.15.38/40/42]

RUTH, master John Forsyth, from Port Glasgow to Charleston, South Carolina, in November 1783. [NAS.E504.22.36]

ST ANDREW OF GLASGOW, master John Brown, arrived in Greenock on 6 October 1728 from Virginia; master James Butcher, from Greenock on 19 December 1729 bound for Virginia. [EEC#554/579]

ST ANDREW, Captain Dunlop, arrived in Annapolis, Maryland, in September 1745, from Orkney on 5 August 1745. [MdGaz#23]

ST ANDREW, a snow, master Thomas Johnston, arrived in Annapolis, Maryland, in August 1747 from Glasgow. [MdGaz#126]

ST ANDREW OF NEW YORK, master Robert Donaldson, from Kirkwall, Orkney, to New York on 2 October 1753. [NAS.E504.26.2]

ST ANDREW, a 150 ton snow, master Arthur Gibbon, from Aberdeen *with passengers* to Kingston, Jamaica, in June 1758. [AJ#535/542]

ST ANDREW, master Richard Hunter, from Greenock to Jamaica in March 1759, [NAS.E504.15.9]

ST ANDREW, master David Scott, from Greenock to St Kitts in January 1779; from Greenock to Jamaica in January 1781; from Greenock to Jamaica in January 1782. [NAS.E504.15.30/33/35]

ST GEORGE OF MONTROSE, master Richard Hartley, from Montrose to Guinea, then Antigua and return by 1754, [NAS.AC7.46.51]; master John Dunbar, in Charleston, South Carolina, during January 1760. [PRO.CO5.510]

ST GEORGE, Captain Cunningham, from Greenock to Jamaica on 1 March 1819. [EEC#16809]

ST JOHNSTON OF PERTH, master Thomas Greig, from Dundee to Philadelphia in August 1764. [NAS.E504.11.5][NAS.CE70.1.4]

ST MUNGO, Captain Hall, from Greenock to Barbados on 21 June 1755. [AJ#390]

ST PAUL OF LONDON, master William Otton, from Dundee to Carolina 20 April 1748. [NAS.E504.11.1]

ST THOMAS OF ARBROATH, master John Wallace, arrived in Montrose on 11 May 1743 from North Potomac, Maryland. [NAS.E504.24.1]

SALLY, Captain Paterson, from Greenock to Jamaica on 26 July 1746. [CM#4026]

SALLY, Captain Hyndman, from Greenock to St Kitts in October 1754; master Archibald Hamilton, from Greenock to St Kitts in March 1756. [AJ#356/425][NAS.E504.15.7]

SALLY OF LEITH, 160 tons, master John Murray, from Leith to Jamaica in January 1763, also in November 1763, and in January 1765. [NAS.E504.22.10/11]

SALLY OF IRVINE, 50 ton brigantine, master William Shaw, arrived in Charleston, South Carolina, on 7 February 1764 via Antigua. [PRO.CO5.511]

SALLY OF DUNDEE, 200 tons, master James Patrick, from Dundee *with* passengers to Grenada on 26 February 1773; master George Greig, from Leith to Grenada in February 1776. [AJ#1308] [NAS.E504.22.20]

SALLY OF GLASGOW, master Gregor McGregor, from Greenock to Tobago in March 1777; from Greenock to Tobago in February 1778; from Greenock to Tobago in February 1779; from Greenock to Tobago in October 1779; from Greenock to St Kitts in January 1782. [NAS.E504.15.27/28/30/32/35]

SALLY, master David Scott, from Greenock to Antigua in October 1782; from Greenock to Barbados in November 1783. [NAS.E504.15.37/38]

SALLY, master James Gilkison, from Port Glasgow to Virginia in March 1786. [NAS.E504.28.40]

SALLY OF KIRKCALDY, master John Douglas, at Kingston, Jamaica, in March 1796. [NAS.AC7.72]

SAMUEL AND MARY OF MARYLAND, master Stephen Handy, arrived in Greenock on 11 July 1722 from Maryland. [EEC#563]

SAMUEL ROBERTSON, 450 tons, Captain Choate, from Glasgow to New York in October 1825; from Greenock to New York in August 1827. [DPCA#1209/1305]

SARAH OF BOSTON, master Henry Aitken, from Kirkwall to Boston, New England, 22 April 1751; master Thomas Potts, from Kirkwall to Boston 13 August 1754. [NAS.E504.26.2]

SATISFACTION, master John Burr, from Greenock to Barbados in November 1783. [NAS.E504.15.38]

SCHAW OF GLASGOW, master Joseph Lindsay, from Greenock to Virginia 1 May 1728. [EEC#489]

SCIPIO OF GLASGOW, master John Lyon, arrived in Dundee from Virginia on 24 December 1732; master John McCunn, arrived in Dundee from Virginia on 24 February 1734. [NAS.CE70.1.2]

SCIPIO, master Andrew Lyon, from Greenock to St Kitts in December 1765. [NAS.E504.15.13]

SCOT OF GLASGOW, a galley, master David Spreul, arrived in Greenock from Virginia in 20 days, on 29 June 1728; from Greenock to Virginia on 10 November 1728. [EEC#510/560]

SCOTIA, Captain Erskine, from Dundee *with passengers* to Kingston, Jamaica, in October 1824. [DPCA#1158]

SCOTSMAN, a 280 ton brig, master John Erskine, from Dundee *with passengers* to Kingston, Jamaica, in November 1825; master Henry Reid, from Dundee to New York on 19 June 1828. [DPCA#1211/1348]

SEAHORSE OF ABERDEEN, 100 tons, master John Thomson, from Aberdeen to Virginia in April 1743; arrived in Aberdeen on 1 February 1744 from Virginia; from Aberdeen in April 1744 from Virginia; arrived in Aberdeen on 29 December 1744 from Virginia; master John Lickley, from Aberdeen in June 1745 via Londonderry to Virginia. [NAS.E504.1.1]

SEAHORSE I, master Jonathan Fowler, from Gravesend via Orkney to Albany and Moose, Hudson's Bay, and return in 1752; to Churchill, Hudson's Bay, and return in 1754; master Joseph Spurrell, from Gravesend via Orkney to Albany and Moose, Hudson's Bay, in 1755, 1756; master William Norton, from Gravesend via Orkney to Albany and Moose, Hudson's Bay, and return in 1757, 1758, 1759, 1760; master Jonathan Fowler, from Gravesend via Orkney to Churchill, Hudson's Bay, and return in 1761, 1762, 1763; master Joseph Richards, from Gravesend voa Orkney to Churchill, Hudson's Bay, and return in 1764. [HBCA#2M121/122]

SEAHORSE II, master John Horner, from Gravesend via Orkney to Albany and Moose, Hudson's Bay, and

return in 1768 and 1769; master William
Christopher, from Gravesend via Orkney to
Churchill and York Factory, Hudson's Bay, in
1771,1774, 1777, 1778, 1779, 1780, and 1781.
[HBCA#2M123/124]

SEAHORSE III, master John Richards, from Gravesend
via Orkney to Moose or York Factory, Hudson's
Bay, in 1782 and 1784, 1786 ; master W. T. Lake,
from Gravesend via Orkney to Moose, Hudson's
Bay, in 1785; master Joshua Turnstall, from
Gravesend via Orkney to Churchill, York Factory,
Hudson's Bay, in 1787, and 1788; master Henry
Hanwell, from Gravesend via Orkney to Churchill
and York Factory, Hudson's bay, in 1790, 1791,
and 1792. [HBCA#2M124/125/126]

SHAKESPEARE, master John Goldie, from Dundee *with
passengers* to Charleston on 18 November 1827.
[DPCA#1311]

SHARP, Captain Bruce, arrived in Maryland from
Glasgow in 1768. [MdGaz#1184]

SHARP OF GREENOCK, master James Lawrie, from
Greenock to Grenada in July 1776; master
Archibald Bog, from Greenock to Jamaica in
August 1777; from Greenock to Jamaica in January
1779. [NAS.E504.15.26/28/30]

SILENCE OF BOSTON, master William Taylor, from
Kirkwall, Orkney Islands, to Boston, New England,
in September 1750. [NAS.E504.26.2]

SILVIA OF LIVERPOOL, master James Clymens, from
Scotland to Jamaica in 1718. [NAS.E508.12.6]

SIMSON, master Henry White, arrived in Annapolis,
Maryland, in June 1763 from Glasgow.
[MdGaz#945]

SISTERS OF GREENOCK, master James Taylor, from Greenock to Nevis, and Savannah, Georgia, in November 1774. [NAS.E504.15.24]

SISTERS, Captain Drummond, from the Clyde to Quebec in August 1798. [EWJ#34]

SKEEN, Captain Bishop, from Leith *with 115 passengers* bound for Halifax and Quebec on 28 March 1819. [EEC#16821]

SPEEDWELL OF IRVINE, master John McLeish, from Greenock to Virginia 17 December 1727; arrived in Greenock on 14 October 1728 from Virginia. [EEC#405/555]

SPEEDWELL OF GLASGOW, master William Campbell, from Greenock to Virginia on 22 February 1728; master William Gammell, arrived in Greenock on 14 October 1728 from Virginia [with 283 hogshead of tobacco]. [EEC#438/556]; 90 tons, master James Colquhoun, arrived in Charleston, South Carolina, on 18 January 1735 from Glasgow, [PRO.CO5.509]

SPEIRS, master John Luke, from Port Glasgow to Barbados in October 1772, master John Lusk, from Port Glasgow to Barbados in October 1773, master John Lamond, from Port Glasgow to Jamaica in January 1776. [NAS.E504.28.21/22/23]

SPOONER OF GLASGOW, master Daniel Graham, from Greenock to St Kitts in October 1774; from Greenock to St Kitts in September 1776; from Greenock to St Kitts in January 1778; from Greenock to St Kitts in November 1778; master John Barbour, from Greenock to St Kitts in February 1781. [NAS.E504.15.24/26/28/30/33]

SPRING OF ABERDEEN, master Peter Grant, from Aberdeen *with15 passengers* bound for Quebec in June 1811, arrived there in August 1811. [NAS.E504.1.24][QG.29.8.1811]

STANHOPE, master Archibald Hastie, from Port Glasgow to Prince Edward Island in April 1784; from Port Glasgow to Oranocke, North Carolina, in December 1784. [NAS.E504.28.37/38]

STIRLING CASTLE, master John Cockburn, arrived in Boston, New England, on 16 April 1766 *with passengers* from Scotland. [PAB]

SUCCESS OF GLASGOW, arrived at the York River, Virginia, in December 1745 from Scotland, wrecked in Chesapeake Bay on 31 December 1745. [MdGaz#38]

SUCCESS OF GLASGOW, a 70 ton snow, master James Robertson, in Charleston, New England, during March 1760. [PRO.CO5.510]

SUCCESS OF ANTIGUA, a 90 ton snow, master Patrick Ogilvie, arrived in Charleston, South Carolina, on 3 January 1767 from Dundee. [PRO.CO5.511]

SUSANNA OF SALTCOATS, master William Service, from Port Glasgow to Virginia in May 1746 [NAS.E504.28.2]

SUSANNAH, Captain Laing, from Greenock to Barbados on 7 December 1751; from Greenock to St Kitts on 6 February 1753; from Greenock to Antigua in December 1753; from Greenock to Barbados in January 1755; Captain Ewing, from Greenock via Cork to Antigua on 3 January 1757; master William Laing, from Greenock to Antigua in January 1755. [AJ#207/267/310/368/470] [NAS.E504.15.12]

SUSANNAH, master Charles Livingston, from Port Glasgow to Virginia in March 1785. [NAS.E504.28.38]

SUSIE, master George Crawford, from Greenock to St Lucia in January 1781. [NAS.E504.15.33]

SWALLOW OF INVERNESS, master David Nevoy, from
Scotland to Jamaica in 1728. [NAS.E508.22.6]

SWALLOW OF BOSTON, master Henry Atkin, from
Kirkwall, Orkney Islands, to Boston, New England,
on 20 March 1748. [NAS.E504.26.2]

SWALLOW OF DUNDEE, 75 tons, master William Hill
from Leith to Grenada in October 1774.
[NAS.E504.22.19]

SWALLOW OF AYR, master David Ninian, from Ayr to
Virginia in September 1785. [NAS.E504.4.8]

SWAN OF DUNBARTON, master John Harrison, from
Port Glasgow to the Caribee Islands on 18 March
1685. [NAS.E72.11]

SWAN OF BOSTON, master Joseph Love, from Virginia
to Glasgow in 1697. [NAS.RD3.92.2]

TAGUS, a brig, Captain Simpson, from Glasgow bound
for St John's, New Brunswick, was wrecked near
Grand Menan on 12 December 1818. [EEC#16799]

TERRY, master Thomas Tolson, from Port Glasgow to
Virginia in January 1784. [NAS/E504.28.37]

THETIS, master James Ramsay, from Port Glasgow to
Virginia in August 1784. [NAS.E504.28.37]

THISTLE OF GLASGOW, master John Orr, from
Greenock to Virginia on 17 February 1741.
[CM#3262]

THISTLE OF PORT GLASGOW, 160 tons, master John
Wilson, arrived in Hampton, Virginia, on 13
November 1738 via Philadelphia, [PRO.CO5.1443];
master Hugh Coulter, arrived in Baltimore,
Maryland, in April 1748, [MdGaz#157]; arrived in
Annapolis, Maryland in July 1749 from the Isle of
Maia, [MdGaz#224]; from Annapolis to Glasgow in
November 1749, [MdGaz#239]; arrived in

Annapolis in July 1751 from Glasgow, [MdGaz#326]; from Annapolis to Glasgow in October 1751, [MdGaz#342]; from Port Glasgow to Maryland in April 1752. [NAS.E504.28.5]; arrived in Annapolis in July 1752 *with 5 passengers* from Glasgow; from Annapolis in October 1752 bound for Glasgow, [MdGaz#377/394]

THISTLE OF GREENOCK, an 80 ton snow, master Alexander Marquis, in Charleston, South Carolina, in January 1767. [PRO.CO5.511]

THOMAS AND BETSEY OF LEITH, master John Stein, from Leith to Jamaica before 1783. [NAS.AC7.59]

THOMAS AND BETTY OF MONTROSE, master Robert Mudie, arrived in Montrose on 6 January 1748 from Virginia; from Montrose to Virginia on 2 May 1748. [NAS.E504.24.1]

THOMSON OF GREENOCK, master Archibald McLarty, from Greenock to Jamaica and St Vincent in February 1777; master Archibald Thomson, from Greenock to Jamaica in November 1777. [NAS.E504.15.27/28]

THREE BROTHERS OF SCITUATE, master William Taylor, from Kirkwall to Boston, New England, 23 August 1751. [NAS.E504.26.2]

THREE FRIENDS OF IRVINE, master Francis Green, arrived in Greenock on 5 November 1728 from Nevis. [EEC#50]

TIBBY, Captain Paterson, from Greenock via Cork to Barbados on 29 May 1756; Captain Archdeacon, from Greenock to the West Indies in November 1757. [AJ#439/515]; master David Andrew, from Greenock to Barbados in November 1760, [NAS.E504.15.10]

TIVERTON MERCHANT OF MONTROSE, 60 tons, master Patrick Ogilvie, arrived in Charleston, South Carolina, on 16 October 1736. [PRO.CO5.510]

TORBAY, master Duncan McLean, from Port Glasgow to Port Roseway, Nova Scotia, in July 1784. [NAS.E504.28.37]

TORTULA, master Hugh Douglas, from Port Glasgow to Virginia in February 1786. [NAS.E504.28.40]

TRAVELLER, a 200 ton brig, Captain Goldie, from Glen Elg *with passengers* to Quebec in July 1819. [EEC#16865]; from Aberdeen *with passengers* to Savannah, Georgia, in February 1824; from Dundee to Savannah and Charleston on 1 September 1825 . [DPCA#1123/1201]

TRAVELLER, a 195 ton brig, from Aberdeen *with passengers* to Montego Bay, Jamaica, in March 1827. [AJ#4128]; Captain Anderson, from Aberdeen via Leith *with passengers* bound for Montego Bay, Jamaica, in October 1828. [S.XII.900]

TRYAL OF IRVINE, 50 tons, master Hugh Brown, arrived in Hampton, Virginia, on 13 June 1740 via St Kitts. [PRO.CO5.1443]

TRYALL OF LEITH, 120 tons, master Alexander Urquhart, arrived in Charleston, South Carolina, on 16 February 1764 from Leith. [PRO.CO5.511]

TUCKER OF GREENOCK, master David Scott, from Greenock to Jamaica in December 1774; master Richard Tucker, from Greenock to Grenada, Dominica and the Bay of Honduras in January 1776. [NAS.E504.15.24/26]

TWO BROTHERS, from Leith to Guinea then the West Indies and return via Holland in 1706. [NAS.CC8.8.83/25]

TWO BROTHERS OF ABERDOUR, master Thomas Arnot, from Leith to Philadelphia in July 1747. [NAS.E504.28.1]

TWO BROTHERS OF KIRKCALDY, a 100 ton brig, master James Ballentine, arrived in Charleston, South Carolina, on 14 March 1766 via Madeira. [PRO.CO5.511]

TWO BROTHERS OF LEITH, master Thomas Arnot, at Charleston, South Carolina, in 1753. [PRO.CO5.510]

TWO BROTHERS OF IRVINE, master Thomas Alexander, from Greenock to Antigua in November 1778; from Greenock to Antigua in December 1779; from Greenock to Antigua in December 1781; from Greenock to Antigua in December 1782. [NAS.E504.15.30/32/35/37]

TWO SISTERS, Captain Pinkerton, from Greenock via the Isle of Maia to Barbados in March 1756. [AJ#428]

ULYSSES OF GREENOCK, master David Scott, from Greenock to Jamaica in January 1776. [NAS.E504.15.26]

UNITED KINGDOM, 544 tons, master John Jamieson, from Glasgow to Kingston, Jamaica, in March 1809. [DPCA#345]

UNION OF WHITEHAVEN, master John Younger, from Greenock to Virginia 13 March 1728; arrived in Greenock on 14 December 1728 from Virginia. [EEC#448/579]

UNION, master John Holliday, from Port Glasgow to Virginia in March 1784. [NAS.E504.28.37]

UNION, master Duncan McNaught, from Greenock to Grenada in February 1785; from Greenock to Grenada in February 1786. [NAS.E504.15.40/42]

UNITY OF DUMFRIES, 60 tons, master James Corbett, arrived in Hampton, Virginia, on 16 May 1738 via St Kitts. [PRO.CO5.1444]

URANIA, a 156 ton brig, master William Mearns, from Dundee to New York on 4 March 1828. [DPCA#1329]

VENERABLE, a 237 ton brig, Captain Lithgow, from Dundee *with passengers* to Charleston, South Carolina, in December 1816. [DPCA#747]

VENUS OF ABERDEEN, master Alexander Begg, from Aberdeen *with 3 passengers* to Quebec in April 1813. [NAS.E504.1.24]

VERNON OF POOLE, 92 tons, from Leith *with 180 Palatine passengers* bound for Philadelphia on 10 June 1747. [NAS.E504.28.2]

VIGILANT, master Francis Hay, from Port Glasgow to St Kitts in October 1783; from Port Glasgow to Grenada in June 1784. [NAS.E504.28.36/37]

VIRGINIA, master Arthur Ryburn, from Leith bound for the Rappahannock River, Virginia, in April 1784. [NAS.E504.22.28]

VIRGINIA PLANTER, arrived in the Patuxent River, Maryland, in June 1765 from Glasgow. [MdGaz#1050]

VRIENDSSCHAAP VAN OSTENDE, master Philip Sanson, from Greenock to St Thomas, Danish West Indies, in December 1782. [NAS,E504.15.37]

WALLACE, master Hugh Moody, from Leith to Jamaica in May 1763; from Greenock via Jamaica to Philadelphia in August 1765; from Greenock to Jamaica in September 1766. [NAS.E504.22.10; 15.13]

WALTER OF GLASGOW, master George Lyon, from Port Glasgow to the West Indies on 24 February 1683. [NAS.E72.19.8]

WALTER OF SALTCOATS, master William Hastie, from Greenock to Barbados and St Lucia in April 1782; master Robert Jack, from Greenock to St Kitts in November 1784; from Greenock to Grenada in September 1785. [NAS.E504.15.36/40/41]

WARRIX, master Hugh Wilson, from Irvine bound for Maryland in March 1774. [NAS.E504.18.8]

WARWICK, master Andrew McVey, from Port Glasgow to Barbados in March 1773, [NAS.E504.28.21]

WESTMORELAND, master Abram Hunter, from Greenock to Jamaica in February 1779. [NAS.E504.15.30]

WESTMORELAND, a 261 ton brig, from Dundee to New York on 18 January 1828. [DPCA#1324/1330]

WHILING WIND, alias the **ENDEAVOUR OF WEYMOUTH**, from Virginia bound for England, captured by a French privateer but then liberated by a Dutch man-o'-war and taken to the Shetland Islands in 1691. [NAS.AC7/9]

WILLIAM OF GREENOCK, master James Hall, arrived in Greenock on 21 August 1728 from Virginia. [EEC#532]

WILLIAM, master Peter Brown, from Port Glasgow to Virginia in August 1784. [NAS.E504.28.37]

WILLIAM, a 173 ton brig, master James Laird, from Aberdeen *with passengers* to Halifax, Nova Scotia, in March 1816. [DPCA#709]

WILLIAM AND ANN, master Andrew Kelly, from Irvine bound for Georgia in January 1770.

[NAS.E504.18.7]; arrived in Savannah on 11 May 1770. [GaGaz:16.5.1770]

WILLIAM AND JAMES OF SALTCOATS, master James Kyler, from Port Glasgow to the West Indies in November 1681. [NAS.E72.19.6]

WILLIAM AND JAMES OF IRVINE, master William Ferrie, from Greenock to Antigua in March 1747. [NAS.E504.15.3][CM#4134]

WILLIAM AND JEAN OF SALTCOATS, master James Glasgow, from Greenock via Madeira to Barbados in January 1745. [NAS.E504.15.2]

WILLIAM AND JOHN OF NEWCASTLE, from Scotland to Barbados in 1716. [NAS.E508.10.6]

WILLIAM AND ROBERT OF RENFREW, master Robert Somervell, arrived in Greenock on 16 October 1728 from Maryland. [EEC#559]

WILLIAM GLEN ANDERSON, a 393 ton barque, from Greenock *with passengers* to New Orleans in November 1827. [DPCA#1318]

WILMINGTON OF CAPE FEAR, 80 tons, PB, master Thomas Murray, from Leith to Jamaica in November 1755. [NAS.E504.22.7]

WOODSTOCK, Captain Clark, from Greenock to Jamaica on 29 January 1819. [EEC#16796]

YOUNG, master John Wallace, from Port Glasgow to North Carolina in August 1784. [NAS.E504.28.37]

..........., Captain Van Der Goast, from Kirkcaldy to the West Indies on 7 September 1685. [NAS.E72.9.21]

..............., from Port Askaig, Islay, *with 129 passengers* bound for America in 1769. [NAS.RH1.2.933/ii]

.......'Leith, 7 December 1736, went out one ship for
       Georgia with a great many servants.' [EEC#1991]

......, Captain Bell, arrived in Boston in February 1766
       from Glasgow. [MdGaz#1070]

.........., a brig, arrived in Newbury, New England, in July
       1784, **with 150 passengers** from Scotland to settle
       in Vermont. [MdGaz#1961]

1768 .. 12, 22, 4, 47, 59, 64,
75, 89, 90, 100,
1769 .. 15, 28, 44, 48, 49,
50, 57, 58, 64, 77,
90, 92, 100, 109,
1770 .. 7, 20, 34, 37, 49, 57,
58, 61, 64, 67, 68,
84, 85, 90, 108,
109,
1771 .. 2, 12, 34, 49, 63, 64,
84, 90, 100,
1772 .. 12, 18, 19, 21, 25,
27, 31, 39, 64, 66,
82, 90, 91, 101,
1773 .. 11, 1, 19, 21, 25, 29,
31, 37, 43, 57, 64,
75, 83, 86, 90, 95,
97, 101, 108,
1774 .. 2, 3, 21, 23, 25, 41,
43, 48, 54, 55, 60,
64, 70, 75, 82, 87,
90, 91, 93, 100,
101, 103, 105, 108,
1775 .. 3, 11, 13, 17, 18, 21,
23, 25, 41, 42, 49,
50, 51, 53, 55, 82,
57, 58, 64, 66, 80,
82, 87, 90, 92,
1776 .. 2 3, 4, 10, 1, 12,
13, 16, 23, 25, 28,
32, 33, 39, 42, 47,
49, 57, 58, 60, 62,
64, 66, 75, 78, 82,
84, 87, 91, 97, 100,
101, 105, 106,
1777 .. 3, 4, 5, 13, 16, 18,
25, 47, 57, 60, 62,
63, 64, 75, 77, 79,
80, 82, 86, 89, 90,
98, 100, 104,
1778 .. 3, 4, 13, 16, 18, 21,
22, 23, 25, 36, 39,
42, 51, 57, 60, 63,
64, 75, 79, 80, 82,
83, 90, 94, 98, 100,
101, 106,
1779 .. 3, 4, 11, 15, 16, 18,
19, 21, 23, 25, 28,
31, 33, 36, 38, 39,
42, 43, 44, 45, 46,
50, 55, 60, 64, 69,
73, 75, 92, 94, 96,
98, 100, 106, 108,
1780 .. 64, 90, 92, 100,
1781 .. 3, 4, 5, 6, 18, 19, 24,
25, 34, 40, 42, 43,
44, 58, 60, 63, 64,
75, 79, 85, 88, 90,
96, 100, 101, 102,
106,

1782 .. 3, 4, 10, 13, 15, 18,
21, 24, 25, 26, 39,
40, 42, 44, 50, 58,
59, 63, 64, 72, 73,
75, 78, 79, 83, 87,
88, 90, 92, 96, 98,
100, 106, 107, 108,
1783 .. 3, 4, 7, 10, 13, 15,
19, 20, 21, 22, 26,
28, 37, 39, 40, 42,
45, 50, 52, 55, 56,
60, 61, 70, 72, 73,
75, 76, 77, 79, 82,
85, 88, 91, 96, 98,
104, 107,
1784 .. 2, 3, 4, 5, 7, 8, 10,
12, 13, 16, 19, 20,
21, 22, 26, 28, 29,
33, 36, 37, 40, 42,
45, 49, 54, 56, 59,
60, 61, 62, 64, 65,
66, 67, 69, 70, 72,
73, 75, 76, 77, 79,
80, 82, 87, 89, 91,
92, 100, 102, 103,
105, 106, 107, 108,
109, 110,
1785 .. 2, 3, 4, 5, 7, 8, 10,
13, 14, 15, 16, 21,
26, 29, 36, 37, 38,
40, 42, 44, 45, 50,
51, 54, 59, 64, 65,
70, 73, 76, 77, 79,
88, 89, 91, 94, 95,
100, 102, 103, 106,
108,
1786 .. 1, 5, 7, 10, 11, 13,
20, 26, 27, 28, 37,
38, 40 42, 44, 50,
51, 52, 60, 61, 63,
64, 68, 69, 72, 78,
79, 83, 84, 85, 86,
91, 94, 98, 100,
106, 105,
1787 .. 5, 13, 26, 38, 39, 40,
45, 59, 64, 68, 76,
79, 100,
1788 .. 12, 15, 64, 100,
1789 .. 1789,
1790 .. 61, 92, 100,
1791 .. 12, 64, 92, 100,
1792 .. 12, 64, 85, 91, 100,
1793 .. 28, 64, 85, 90, 91,
92, 95,
1794 .. 64, 90, 92,
1795 .. 11, 13, 54, 64, 76,
80, 90,
1796 .. 64, 90, 92, 98,
1797 .. 64, 90, 92,

1798 .. 34, 37, 48, 52, 56,
64, 90, 92, 100,
1799 .. 64, 90, 92, 99,
1800 .. 64, 90, 92,
1801 .. 48, 64, 90,
1802 .. 23, 64, 90,
1803 .. 23, 64, 90,
1804 .. 23, 64, 90,
1805 .. 30, 64, 80, 90,
1806 .. 64, 90,
1807 .. 33, 64, 71, 90,
1808 .. 3, 10, 11, 13, 14, 33,
48, 69, 70, 90,
1809 .. 4, 64, 90, 106,
1810 .. 39, 56, 64, 90,
1811 .. 22, 33, 34, 55, 72,
88, 101,
1812 .. 4, 11, 20, 33, 64, 76,
86, 89, 90,
1813 .. 33, 90, 107,
1814 .. 33, 90,
1815 .. 6, 20, 36, 44, 72, 85,
90,
1816 .. 27, 33, 40, 43, 46,
48, 49, 52, 63, 69,
92, 107, 108,
1817 .. 7, 29, 33, 36, 44, 45,
48, 52, 54, 66, 85,
86, 90,
1818 .. 33, 90, 103,
1819 .. 5, 9, 11, 23, 30, 38,
40, 42, 46, 54, 56,
68, 69, 71, 72, 73,
74, 81, 90, 97, 101,
105, 109,
1820 .. 33, 38, 42, 54, 66,
90,
1821 .. 2, 33, 51, 54, 70, 90,
95,
1822 .. 33, 90,
1823 .. 9, 10, 16, 32, 33, 67,
90,
1824 .. 7, 9, 10, 20, 25, 41,
45, 48, 54, 62, 72,
78, 79, 80, 85, 90,
99, 105,
1825 .. 10, 18, 20, 38, 45,
49, 56, 73, 79, 90,
95, 98, 99, 105,
1826 .. 16, 18, 54, 79, 90,
93,
1827 .. 2, 11, 12, 19, 26, 34,
35, 36, 45, 48, 49,
58, 69, 76, 90, 91,
93, 94, 98, 100,
105, 109,
1828 .. 3, 18, 22, 27, 28, 35,
45, 49, 57, 58, 67,
71, 90, 91, 95, 99,
105, 107, 108,